CBT Workbook for Teens

Skills and Activities to Help Your Son to Conquer Negative Thinking, Anxiety and Depression. How to Manage his Moods and Boost Self- Esteem to Stress Reduction, Shyness and Social Anxiety.

Rebecca Thompson

© **Copyright 2020 by Rebecca Thompson - All rights reserved.**

The content contained within this book may not be reproduced, duplicated, or transmitted without direct written permission from the author or the publisher.

Under no circumstances will any blame or legal responsibility be held against the publisher, or author, for any damages, reparation, or monetary loss due to the information contained within this book. Either directly or indirectly. You are responsible for your own choices, actions, and results.

Legal Notice:

This book is copyright protected. This book is only for personal use. You cannot amend, distribute, sell, use, quote or paraphrase any part, or the content within this book, without the consent of the author or publisher.

Disclaimer Notice:

Please note the information contained within this document is for educational and entertainment purposes only. All effort has been executed to present accurate, up to date, and reliable, complete information. No warranties of any kind are declared or implied.

Readers acknowledge that the author is not engaging in the endearing of legal, financial, medical, or professional advice. The content within this book has been derived from various sources.

Please consult a licensed professional before attempting any techniques outlined in this book.

By reading this document, the reader agrees that under no circumstances is the author responsible for any losses, direct or indirect, which are incurred as a result of the use of the information contained within this document, including, but not limited to, — errors, omissions, or inaccuracies.

TABLE OF CONTENTS

Introduction..9

Chapter 1: CBT...13

1.1 Cognitive Behavioral Therapy, what it is?

1.2 Different types of CBT

1.3 The Principles of CBT

1.4 The Benefits of CBT

1.5 Improve the areas of your life with CBT:

- Relationships

-School/Work

-Spirituality

-Health

-Recreation

-Goal Setting

-Exercise

Chapter 2: Why Mindset it's so important........................33

2.1 Mindset, What it is?

2.2 The Right Mentality and Attitude In Life

2.3 Differences between Growth Mindset and Fixed Mindset

2.4 The Fixed Mindset

2.5 The Growth Mindset

2.6 Developing a Mindset Capable of Guiding You Toward Your Goals

2.7 Exercises

2.8 Face Your Fears

2.9 Exposure

Chapter 3: Beliefs...48

3.1 What Are Beliefs?

3.2 Perfectionism

3.3 Approval: Do you really need it?

How and Why Your Beliefs Act and Affect the Way You Think

3.4 Recognize Your Beliefs

3.5 Change your Negative Beliefs

3.6 Commitment and Determination

3.7 Exercises

3.8 Organize Your Thoughts

3.9 Defining the Objective

Chapter 4: Values..79

4.1 What Are Values?

4.2 Recognize all your value

4.3 The importance of values

4.4 How values can influence everything about us?

4.5 Dilemmas

4.6 How to Understand the values in our life

4.7 Why Values can guide us

4.8 Exercise

4.9 The Pyramid of Your Values

Chapter 5: Master Negative Thinking..............................90

5.1 The arise of negative thinking

5.2 Negative Thoughts

5.3 What Feeds Our Negative Thoughts?

5.4 The effects of Negative Thoughts in our life

5.5 Five Negative Thinking Habits

"I Can't" Habit

"All or Nothing" Habit

"I Should, You Should" Habit

"It's Not Fair" Habit

"Mind Reading" Habit

Eliminating Negative Thoughts

Hypothesizing

Visualization

Exercises

5.6 Focus on Your Strengths

5.7 Reframe Your Thoughts

5.8 Question Your Thoughts

Chapter 6: Beat and conquer Anxiety........................111

6.1 Anxiety, what it is?

6.2 Why Anxiety control our life

6.3 When Does Anxiety Manifest?

6.4 When Does Anxiety Affect Us?

6.5 Different Types of Anxiety

6.6 GAD: Generalized Anxiety Disorder

6.7 Phobias

6.8 Shyness

6.9 How to Eliminate Anxiety

6.10 Parents

Exercises

6.11 Breathing Exercises

6.12 Meditation

Chapter 7: Emotions and Moods..................................125

7.1 What Are Moods?

7.2 How Our Moods Influence Our Choices and Life

7.3 Important Moods

7.4 How to Manage Our Moods in Our Favor

 Exercises

7.5 Mood Awareness Write

Chapter 8: Boost Your Self-Esteem................................133

8.1 What Is Self-Esteem?

8.2 What Influences Self-Esteem?

8.3 Low Self-Esteem High Self-Esteem

8.4 How We Evaluate Ourselves

8.5 Other People's View and the Effect on Our Self-Esteem Social Comparison

8.6 How to Increase Low Self-Esteem

    1. Problem Solving

    2. Self-Talk

    3. Self-Control Self-Actualization

Chapter 9: New Thoughts..149

Exercises

9.1 Affirmations

9.2 Create a Let It Go Phrase Shift to a Growth Mindset

Chapter 10: New Behaviors..154

10.1 Recognize the Behaviors You Want to Change

10.2 Behaviors That Are Beneficial But You Avoid

10.3 Positive Reinforcement

10.4 Accountability

Chapter 11: Creating New Objectives?........................164

11.1 Steps for Creating New Objectives

11.2 Why Set New Objectives?

11.3 Creating an Action Plan

Conclusion..172

References..174

Introduction

Teens are considered naturally moody, temperamental, and defiant. They want independence but still need to learn how to be responsible enough to handle that independence. For many, the teen years are a struggle. There are many choices they need to make on their own, there is constant pressure to behave and perform a specific way, and they are just beginning to learn who they are and who they want to be. The pressure they feel from others resonates deep within their minds and can paralyze them.

Unfortunately, teens are never directly taught how to handle emotions or how to react appropriately in social settings. While they may be told what not to do, there is often no alternative provided for what they should do instead. Teens are faced with making a number of tough choices throughout their adolescent years. While some breeze through these years, many suffer silently.

The number of teens that hide their anxiety, depression, and insecurity is overwhelming. These years are meant to be the best of their lives. For many, they are a constant battle.

The way they think about themselves during these years is how they will view themselves as adults. The way they cope with their emotions, thoughts, and the behaviors they exhibit in these years will either hinder or propel their success. What many teens lack is the ability to identify and make a connection between their thoughts, emotions, and behaviors.

While they focus on studying, making friends, and attending football games, they neglect to question their thoughts or emotions. They may

constantly fight off a negative self-image, limiting belief systems, and intense feelings of fear simply because they don't want to address them or they just don't know how.

Cognitive Behavioral Therapy can provide teens with the knowledge and tools they need to let go of what is holding them back. This type of therapy addresses the thoughts, behaviors, and emotions that can cause a teen to act out of control, withdraw from friends, and fall behind in school. When you begin Cognitive Behavioral Therapy, you gain an understanding of your negative thoughts, the power they have, and how you can regain control over them.

What to expect:

This book is designed to introduce you to the practices and techniques common in Cognitive Behavioral Therapy. You will gain an understanding of how your thoughts, emotions, and behaviors are all connected and how they can be causing you to feel anxious, depressed, shy, and lost. Throughout this book, you will be introduced to key aspects of your life that you will want to carefully consider and answer questions about. You will learn how to identify what is truly important to you, the beliefs and views you have about yourself, and how to overcome negative thoughts and anxiety.

Each chapter covers a specific topic that will, in the end, allow you to set clear goals and make necessary changes that will not only affect your teenage years but will impact your adult life. As you read through the information, refrain from skipping ahead. Go through each chapter and answer the questions as they arise.

It is helpful to have a designated journal as you go through each chapter. This will give you a place to answer questions and more importantly will give you a place to track your progress. Your journal provides you with a reference guide that you can turn to remember what you truly want out of your life.

For Teens

A lot of the information in these pages will benefit you in various ways. Be open and willing to follow through the exercises and keep track of the questions you answer. The material will help you better understand what is causing you to struggle in many areas of your life and will give you the confidence that you can overcome any challenges you face.

For Parents

While this book is geared toward helping teens overcome the struggles they are facing, don't ignore how some of the information in these pages can benefit you as well. Work with your teen to complete the exercise and practice the techniques. Many of the chapters have additional sections specifically for you. You will find tips that can help your child adopt new thoughts and behaviors. You will also find ways to identify when your teen might be struggling and solutions for tackling big emotions and uncomfortable situations.

Use this book to not only encourage your teen to develop the skills that will benefit them throughout their lives but will allow them to grow into confident and successful men and women.

Chapter 1: What Is CBT?

Cognitive Behavioral Therapy was developed in the 1960s by Aaron T. Beck (History of Cognitive Behavior Therapy, n.d.). His work focused on treating those with depression when he noticed similarities in the thought patterns these patents had. Not only did he notice patterns in their thoughts, but he also noticed that when these negative thoughts were evaluated by the patient, they were able to adjust their thinking to focus on the truths and facts of the situation. They were able to combat the negative thoughts, which left them feeling more in control and happier about themselves, the people around then, and the way they viewed the world.

What Is Cognitive Behavioral Therapy?

Cognitive Behavioral Therapy is a form of psychotherapy that focuses on how we think, feel, and behave. These three factors shape who we are, the relationships we have, and how we live our lives. Cognitive Behavioral Therapy is a way to help individuals learn to take control of their life and live in alignment with what matters most to them. It has been an effective way to help treat a variety of psychiatric, psychological, physical, and additional health conditions.

Those with a diagnosed medical condition benefit significantly from this form of therapy. The practices, techniques, and tools used in sessions, however, are ones that can help benefit just about anyone who is suffering from negative thoughts, behaviors, and emotions. Adults, teens, and children can use Cognitive Behavioral tools to overcome debilitating anxiety, severe depression, or big emotions they are struggling to make sense of. Teens especially can learn valuable skills that they can carry with them for the rest of their lives. This can aid in the success they have in school, work, and relationships.

Cognitive Behavioral Therapy focuses on learning to stay in the present moment, set goals, and understand how the thought process affects behaviors. Though it is a short-term treatment, it offers long- term positive results. Through this type of therapy, you learn to reprogram your thinking patterns. You also learn the connections that are made between your emotions, thoughts, and behaviors.

Cognitive Behavioral Therapy combines a number of techniques so that the patient can reach their specific goals. Each session includes reviewing progress or concerns. The patient is then given homework

that will help them move forward to overcome that negative or dysfunctional thinking. Cognitive Behavioral Therapy is used in varying ways, each focusing on the negative thoughts, behaviors, and emotions that can hold you back.

Types of CBT

- Acceptance and Commitment Therapy (ACT)

Acceptance and Commitment Therapy combines traditional behavior therapy and Cognitive Behavior Therapy in an action-oriented approach to resolve behavioral and psychological issues. This approach involves individuals learning to accept their feelings and thoughts as opposed to avoiding them. Goals are established so that the individual can begin to make the necessary changes and learn how to modify their behaviors so that they can live more fulfilling lives. This type of Cognitive Behavior Therapy is an effective way for individuals to address their fears, reduce stress, and confront their anxieties. The focus is on the way you speak to yourself and view the world around you as a result of a traumatic event or occurrence. You begin to fully understand what is holding you back, why it continues to hold you back, and are taught strategies to overcome and persevere.

- Dialectical Behavior Therapy (BDT)

This type of Cognitive Behavioral Therapy is often used to help individuals with severe mood or personality disorders. Those struggling with forming healthy relationships or who struggle in social settings can greatly benefit from Dialectical Behavior Therapy. The focus of this therapy is providing support to the individual. You learn to focus on your unique strengths to build up self-esteem. You discuss

the limiting beliefs, thoughts, and assumptions that run through your mind when in different situations. Specific goals are set to help you identify big emotions you struggle to process appropriately. You learn how to change the way you react to these emotions and how to change your negative thoughts patterns when confronting these emotions so you gain control over them. DBT often combines mindfulness practices with effective thought recognition techniques so that individuals can regulate their emotions and learn new ways to approach distressing or uncomfortable emotions and situations.

- Mindfulness-Based Cognitive Therapy (MBCT)

Mindfulness-Based Cognitive Therapy teaches you how to become more aware of your thoughts. By raising your awareness, you are able to effectively identify negative thoughts and can then learn how to reword and change them to be more empowering and helpful. This type of therapy is one that will provide you with a number of skills and techniques that can be valuable throughout the course of your life.

- Cognitive Processing Therapy (CPT)

Cognitive Processing Therapy is often used to help those suffering from severe mental disorders such as post-traumatic stress disorder. Through this therapy, individuals focus on how they process traumatic events and how they may distort the event. The look closely at the coping skills that have been implemented to deal with the thoughts, behaviors, and emotions when the event is remembered. You learn to identify the inaccurate thoughts that run through your mind and address the unwanted behaviors you exhibit when trying to work through those thoughts when they arise. You learn to evaluate situations to find the truths in them so that you can rewire your thinking and gain control and overcome the events that occurred to you.

Throughout this book, you will be provided with a range of techniques and exercises that are commonly used in many of these types of Cognitive Behaviour Therapy. The most effective strategies for identifying limiting beliefs, negative thoughts, and uncomfortable emotions are explained. You will also be taught how you can begin to solve and eliminate these components that are holding you back. Working through each of the exercises will provide you with the foundation you need to set specific goals that will empower you to reach your full potential.

CBT Principles

The main goal of Cognitive Behavioral Therapy is to help you learn how to resolve the mental blocks, behaviors, and emotions that hold you back. During your teenage years, you will be confronted with unavoidable situations where you will struggle with making the best choices. This can result in unpleasant and big reactions to the choices you make as you either regret the choice or wished you knew how to change the way you react in situations.

Cognitive Behavioral Therapy is effective in helping teens overcome limiting behaviors and thoughts because of its core principles.

1.Active Participation

Participants are expected to take an active role in the sessions. They help define goals, create action plans, and practice techniques that will move them forward. Being active involves being aware that work will need to be done to overcome what holds them back. It also involves being open and willing to try suggested exercises and techniques that can help change the way they think, feel, and act. Though some exercises may give immediate results and help them recognize where

thoughts are faulty or where behavior needs to be changed, some techniques will need to be practiced. Remaining positive and actively addressing what you want to change will lead you to find great success.

2.Goal-Oriented

When an individual decides to begin Cognitive Behavioral Therapy, there are specific problems that they want to address and resolve. Stating these problems is the first step to managing them. Goals are clear and matched with specific treatment techniques that will allow them to manage and accomplish what they want. Goals should be personal to you, and you need to have a strong desire to achieve them. As mentioned, changing your behaviors and thoughts will take practice and you might not always get it right on the first try.

Having a clearly defined goal will keep you committed to the process.

3. Focus on the Present Moment

Cognitive Behavioral Therapy is uniquely different from many other forms of therapy because it focuses on the present moment. The goal is to help individuals recognize their thoughts and emotions and how they impact their behaviors now. There is not much focus placed on what occurred earlier in childhood unless addressing these matters will lead the individual toward their goal. By focusing on what occurs in the here and now, the individual is able to feel more empowered and confident in the ability to control the factors that they face on a daily basis as opposed to dealing with events that occurred in the past.

4. Provide You with the Necessary Tools

Cognitive Behavioral Therapy aims to teach individuals how they can manage their problems by utilizing the skills they already possess.

CBT teaches one to strengthen these skill sets and to look at things with a different perspective so that they are able to apply new techniques to situations that have been holding them back. These skills and techniques are valuable tools that individuals can tap into for the rest of their lives to overcome even the most devastating experiences.

5. Relapse Prevention

Individuals are specifically taught and made aware of the key factors that can trigger unwanted experiences like anxiety and depression. By understanding the factors that can contribute to these intense mental blocks, an individual can recognize early signs of the symptoms that can lead to a relapse. When these signs are recognized, the individual can make the necessary adjustments and implement the right tools that will allow them to avoid falling into becoming trapped by their emotions or thoughts.

6. Time-Limited

Cognitive Behavioral Therapy tends to address and successfully help individuals reach their goals in a short amount of time. Some individuals may find themselves able to move past their roadblocks in just a session or two. These shorter treatment plans give individuals more hope and assurance that they will be able to overcome what has been holding them back.

7. Structured

Cognitive Behavioral Therapy provides individuals with a predictable order of steps to take that are necessary for achieving their specific goal in a short amount of time. If you are seeing a therapist, sessions will often begin by addressing the specific problem, going over a tool

or technique to help confront the problem, and assigning a homework assignment the individual is to complete before the next session. When they meet again, the session will begin with a review of how the homework assignment went, what changes can be made, and a new homework assignment is given. Sessions are straightforward and organized, which is what makes it such an effective way to help individuals better manage their thoughts, emotions, and behaviors.

8. Addresses Negative Thoughts

Gaining control over one's thoughts is a key focus in Cognitive Behavioral Therapy. Negative thinking can be the root cause of many problems and setbacks individuals are dealing with. Cognitive Behavioral Therapy provides individuals specific ways to identify, reverse, and create new thoughts that are empowering and positive. Addressing the negative thoughts the individual may or may not be aware of is how they will be able to adopt more helpful ways of thinking.

9. Incorporates Various Techniques

Cognitive Behavioral Therapy utilizes a number of techniques in the session and homework assignments. Individuals may learn a list of ways they can help improve their life. This can include meditation, breathing exercises, relaxation training, and exposure therapy, among others. These techniques (which will be discussed in greater detail along with others) are tested by the individual so that they can find the right techniques that are the most beneficial for them.

How Can CBT Benefit You?

The goal of Cognitive Behavioral Therapy is to help you understand your thought process and thought patterns. New patterns are developed by evaluating and assessing past experiences, identifying triggers, and setting goals that will allow you to master your thoughts and live a more fulfilling life.

As a teen, this may sound like a complex process. But, from a young age, we learn to behave in accordance with our thoughts. In this day and age, it has never been more vital for teens to learn how to identify and redirect their negative thinking.

There are many things that Cognitive Behavioral Therapy can help you manage and take control of such as:

- How to identify your negative thoughts.
- How to process big emotions.
- How to manage anger.
- How to process grief or loss.
- How to overcome trauma.
- How to have better sleep.
- How to work through difficult relationships.

The main benefit, however, is recognizing how your thoughts affect your emotions and behavior. It strives to strengthen your ability to identify negative thoughts and re-program your thought process so that you can handle stress, anxiety, fear, and other challenges better.

How CBT Can Improve Areas of Your Life

Teens have to process a number of big emotions and situations. Many of these can be easily faced and many can lead to poor decisions and low self-esteem. Teens who undergo Cognitive Behavioral Therapy often find a solution to their anxiety that surrounds things like test- taking, time management, speaking in class, socializing, and setting goals that will lead to a successful life well after they leave high school. All areas of your life can be impacted by Cognitive Behavioral Therapy.

Relationships

Relationships have a direct impact on the way you think of yourself and the world around you. Feeling connected with others is essential for social development, but having these deep connections can strengthen the image you have of yourself. Relationships are those that you have with your parents, siblings, friends, or significant other. They can also include the relationship you have with coworkers and teachers.

When looking at the relationship area of your life, take note of the following key aspects.

- Which relationships are going well for you?
- What parts of these relationships are working out well?
- Where are you struggling in your relationships?
- How is your communication in these relationships?
- Do you spend enough time with the people in these relationships?
- What is your connection like with these people?

Cognitive Behavioral Therapy can help you recognize how you speak to others and how to boost your self-confidence to build more meaningful relationships. It can walk you through how you feel others view you and how other people's words and actions can affect the way you treat yourself and your behavior. You will learn how to build a clear vision of yourself that will help you feel more comfortable and confident being yourself around others.

Create a list of all the individuals (friends, family, siblings, and others) you have a relationship with. How would you like to improve these relationships? Ask yourself how your thoughts, feelings, or behaviors may be affecting these relationships (good and bad).

School/Work

Some teens are entering or are already in the work field while also attending school. Other teens are focused on school and extracurricular activities. In either case, this is a significant area of life for teens. Since school will be the place you spend much of your young adult life, it is essential that this area of life makes you happy. When you suffer from anxiety, depression, or other stresses, you will feel less ecstatic about this area of your life.

Teens should be taught to find meaning in their school work, extracurricular activities, and the jobs they may have during these years. This will allow them to graduate to pursue careers that give their life more meaning and happiness. Some teens are not

challenged enough to become enthusiastic about this area; others feel insecure, anxious, or afraid of their potential (or, in their mind, lack of) to truly excel in this area.

When considering this area of your life, look at:

- What your thoughts on having a quality education are.
- What classes in school do you enjoy most?
- Are there classes you should put more effort into?
- What other activities are you involved in?
- Which of these activities do you enjoy?
- How much do you enjoy your current job?

- What career are you thinking of pursuing after high school?

Spirituality

Spirituality is what makes us feel connected with the world around us. Some people find their spirituality by following a religion, others find it through yoga and meditation, and some find this connection when they are in nature. Spirituality is what gives us more meaning and purpose and reminds us that we are part of something much bigger than just what we see and experience in our daily lives.

When thinking about this area of your life, ask yourself:

- What is important to you?
- What is it that you really care about?
- Are your actions purposeful?
- Do you feel connected to something meaningful?
- What would you like others to say about you?

Health

Living a healthy lifestyle may not be a major concern when you are a teen. Not many are concerned about how all the fast food and chips will impair them in the future. But, poor food choices, lack of exercise, and skipping sleep all impact our mental health as well as physical health. Individuals who commit to a healthy lifestyle are often able to overcome all kinds of difficulties both emotionally and physically. "Healthy" is different for everyone but involves moving your body, eating right, getting enough sleep, and managing stress appropriately.

Questions to ask yourself when thinking about your health:

- How would you consider your overall health?
- Are there any health problems you currently have that affect your life?
- Do you exercise or move your body during the week?
- Do you have any aches or pains when you exercise?
- Does your mood affect your motivation to exercise?
- How would you consider your diet?
- Are your eating habits influenced by your mood or thoughts?
- What is your sleep like?
- Do you find your thoughts keep you awake?
- Are there things that happen in the day that keep you from getting proper sleep?
- What aspects of your health would you like to see improve?

Recreation

While there are many responsibilities teenagers must have, they should also have a number of activities that bring them joy or help them feel recharged. While many teens are involved in a variety of sports or extracurricular activities, many exert themselves in thes

areas not because it brings them ultimate joy but to please those around them. It is important that the things you spend your time doing are things that you really enjoy. While you may not want to face your parents or teacher's disapproval, taking up hobbies or spending time doing things you want to learn more about or just enjoy are things that will impact your overall happiness. This is an important lesson to learn at a young age. As you get older, you will often find it harder to make time for the things you enjoy; you may find you go off to college just to pursue a future your parents or community expected you to pursue. In the end, you may find yourself pleasing everyone else, but you find that you are not happy or feel like you are not doing what you are meant to do.

When you do not make time for recreational activities you enjoy, you may fall into the habit of doing for others, which results in being unclear about who you are. You will often find yourself sticking to this pattern as you get older. You might ignore the things you truly want to pursue in order to follow what everyone else expects you to. This can result in developing anxiety, depression, and chronic stress.

When thinking about this area of your life, carefully consider and answer the following questions.

- What are some things you enjoy doing?

- Do you feel you have enough time to do the things you enjoy doing?

- Have you noticed that your mood or thoughts have kept you from doing activities you used to enjoy?

Goal Setting

Being able to set and take action to achieve goals is something many teens are never taught to do. You may know how to start and finish projects or homework on time, but you may not know how you can set your own goals or take action to improve the areas of your life you want to improve.

When it comes to goal setting, you want to think about the things that you have wanted to achieve. When have you decided you were going to accomplish something and then took action to work toward accomplishing those things?

Are there times where you may want to achieve a goal but never actually got started?

As a teen, this can work to improve a grade in one of your classes, working to make the varsity team, or finding a job after school. Many teens need an authority figure to motivate or remind them of what they should be doing. If they do not get this external motivation, they are unaware that they have the ability to motivate themselves internally.

Setting goals and taking action on those goals is a skill that will lead you to more success in life. Being able to self-motivate and take initiative on your own to accomplish things will transform you into an adult who is unafraid to face challenges, try new things, or have big dreams. One of the things most teens never understand is that there are so many possibilities in the world, but they get stuck thinking about where they grew up, how they were raised, or the small town that encompasses them is all there is.

Do not be afraid to set goals for yourself. You can begin by setting small goals. You can begin by looking at the areas of your life and identifying where you want to see improvements. Once you have

pinpointed the area you want to work on, you can begin to understand what actions you can take to see the changes and reach the goals you set.

Exercise

Consider each of the areas of your life.

Give each area a rating from 1-10, 1 meaning you think this area needs significant improvement and 10 meaning you are completely satisfied with this area and wouldn't change a thing about it.

AREAS OF LIFE

RATING

RELATIONSHIP

SCHOOL/WORK

SPIRITUALITY

HEALT

RECREATION

GOAL SETTING

Chapter 2: Mindset

When faced with a problem, do you tend to think you can find a solution, or do you immediately think the task impossible? Our mindset is what allows us to see opportunities when they arrive. Our mindset can also install a level of defeat that holds us back, makes us fearful, and hinders our ability to be successful throughout our lives. Over time, as our mindset develops fully, it is our mindset that determines the person we become. Your mindset can define who you are. You can let your mindset burden you or your mindset can be the key factor in the shifts you need to make to excel.

What Is Mindset?

Mindset is the way you think about yourself or believe in your qualities, such as your intelligence, physical capabilities, and talents. It impacts how we approach challenges in our lives. Mindset is what allows someone to preserve and be resilient in reaching their goals no matter what complications or obstacles they may face on the way.

For a teen, developing a healthy mindset can affect grades, relationships, and all areas of your life. The right mindset will help you to identify and pursue things you are passionate about. More importantly, the mindset you develop in these teenage years can allow you to succeed after high school.

Having the Right Attitude and Mentality in Life

Developing the right mindset can lead to a life that allows you to truly succeed. When faced with a problem, do you tend to look at it as a way to learn and grow, or do you immediately think it is impossible and that you will be judged or criticized if you are unable to solve the problem correctly? The first mindset allows you to face problems with optimism. It results in your ability to try new things, set goals, and step outside your comfort zone. When we are unable to approach our problems with a mindset of empowerment, we automatically think that a lack of abilities and knowledge makes it impossible to solve or even face challenges.

Fixed Mindset vs. Growth Mindset

There are many categories your mindset can fall into. The two most common are a fixed mindset or a growth mindset. Children tend to naturally have a growth mindset, but as they grow older and face new challenges, this mindset can shift and become fixed. Understanding the components of each and how they affect all areas of your life will allow you to identify where you need to make a shift in your mindset so that you can grow and accomplish the goals you set for yourself.

Fixed Mindset

A fixed mindset can leave us on the defensive. Individuals with a fixed mindset often focus on their failures. They are unable to accept constructive criticism and therefore are unable to make the progress they are capable of to improve their skills and life. Individuals with a fixed mindset tend to think in a black-and-white pattern. They are either smart or intelligent, they are either accepted or rejected, they are either a winner or a failure.

A fixed mindset will result in constantly looking for validation. Children adopt this mindset when they are constantly praised for being or looking smart instead of being praised for their eagerness to learn. As these children become teens, they become fixed on the idea that they will be judged on how smart they are if they do not look or meet the expectations imposed by their parents or teachers. They then fear being a disappointment when they do not live up to those expectations.

They do not focus on the work they put into accomplishing something; they only focus on the end result. Those with a fixed mindset will often have thoughts that focus on:

- Not being able to increase their intelligence.

- Thinking that individuals only have a set amount of intelligence that can not be changed.

- The notion that there is not much that can be done to improve your capabilities or change who you are.

- Believing that the talents you have are the only ones you are capable of. You cannot acquire new talents or skills even if you are presented with an opportunity to learn them

Growth Mindset

A growth mindset is one that motivates you to improve, learn, and work harder for the things you want to accomplish. Those with a growth mindset love to learn new things, welcome challenges, and have an unshakeable desire to learn more. Those with a growth mindset are not afraid to try new things because they are not afraid to fail. Failure to an individual with a growth mindset is an opportunity to learn. New opportunities can come from these failures and a growth mindset allows individuals to seek out these opportunities.

Everything is a learning experience when you have a fixed mindset. Children who are encouraged to explore their surroundings, work through challenging situations, and learn from their experiences, will be more likely to develop a growth mindset. When these children become teens they are able to enjoy the process of learning. They feel a great deal of accomplishment for putting in the work and are not just focused on the end result. They understand that things may not work

out the way they intend, but they are able to evaluate what they do, and therefore, are able to learn from mistakes and make the necessary improvements.

Keep in mind that a growth mindset does not mean you think that they can achieve whatever you want just by saying it. Instead, you understand that you must work hard, learn the skills, and educate yourself to be able to reach the goals you set. You understand that if you want to achieve anything, you need to practice and continuously look for ways to improve.

Someone with a growth mindset will have thoughts that include:

- Knowing that they are able to change who they are.
- Knowing that they can learn and increase their intelligence.
- There are many ways in which you can develop your talents and obtain new skills.

Developing a Mindset Capable of Guiding You Toward Your Goals

Developing a growth mindset allows you to set goals and achieve those goals. With a growth mindset, you understand that you are able to live up to your highest potential. This potential, however, is unlimited. There is no ceiling that limits how far you can go. With a growth mindset, you understand that learning and deepening your understanding of the things that interest you will take effort, but that effort is worth the time and energy.

Setting goals is an important step to encouraging a growth mindset. But the focus should not be solely on the end result. Focusing on the process and celebrating the victories along the way is what matters most. Instead of focusing on getting an A in a class, focus on all the new information you are receiving, focus on how this information can benefit you outside the classroom, and focus on the work you are putting in. The end result may not be what you hope for, but it is the steps you take to get the results that matter most. Working hard for something and feeling proud of your efforts is far more important.

Think of your mindset as having its own voice. Your mindset will affect the way you talk to yourself and the more positive your mindset is the more positively you will speak internally to yourself. There are many phrases you might be saying to yourself that undermines what you are actually capable of. Spotting these fixed mindset phrases can help you shift your dialogue to one that is growth-oriented. If you catch yourself focusing on what you are lacking when you face a problem, this is an indication of a fixed mindset. When you notice you are focused on the skills or knowledge that you do not have, you can use this to formulate a plan to acquire the skills or knowledge you do not yet possess.

Switching the way you approach these phrases will encourage you to push yourself and stretch your skills to learn and accomplish what you set out to do. You can challenge these phrases by reframing the dialog you have with yourself. Instead of focusing on not having the skills or knowledge, tell yourself that you can learn and improve on the skills you have that will allow you to accomplish your goals. Instead of worrying about the mistakes you will make or failing at accomplishing your goals, focus on the fact that everyone fails and that if you fail, you will have learned a lot of valuable lessons along the way.

It is one thing to change your internal dialog to move toward a growth mindset, but you can reinforce these thoughts more effectively with actions. For you to truly believe that you are capable of more and growing, you need to take actions that support these thoughts. Practice what you say, set a goal to gather more information by reading more on a specific topic, or set the time aside to practice the skills you want to learn. When you start acting in accordance with your thoughts, your mindset will continue to grow and encourage you to do more.

Exercises

Face Your Fears

What is one thing that you have been wanting to do but fear has been holding you back?

Consider what is the worst thing that can happen?

How likely is it that this outcome will occur?

If this outcome were to occur, how would that really affect the person you are?

Now think of the opposite outcome.

What steps can you take to better ensure this outcome would occur?

Consider things you could do that would be outside of your comfort zone.

Exposure

When it comes to shifting your mindset, one of the things you can do to have a growth mindset is to gradually expose yourself to the things you want to do but let fear or anxiety hold you back.

Consider situations where you tend to have a more negative or fixed mindset.

What situation do you avoid because of a fixed mindset of not believing in yourself or your abilities?

How can you face the fears you have about these situations?

Create a list of small steps you can take that will allow you to feel more comfortable and confident in these settings.

1.

2.

3.

4.

5.

Choose one thing from this list and actually follow through and do it.

Chapter 3: Beliefs

Beliefs begin to develop at a young age. We often do not recognize the negative or positive beliefs we hold until much later in life. These beliefs will have a major impact on all areas of your life and will affect the way you approach the people you encounter and the situations you face.

What Are Beliefs?

Beliefs are the core assumptions or thoughts you form about yourself and the world around you. These inner beliefs tend to playback over and over throughout the course of your life. We take these beliefs as facts and assume they are true without really questioning where they manifest from or what has contributed to their formation. They will affect the way you view the world around you. You can either develop a belief system that helps you feel empowered, confident, and capable, or you can develop a set of beliefs that makes you cynical, defeated, and made to feel unimportant.

What one must understand is that these beliefs do not have to be fixed in place. Our core beliefs can be completely wrong, and we can change them! Some examples of untrue beliefs:

- Everyone is better than me.

- I'm stupid.
- Everyone is so selfish.
- Everyone takes advantage of me.

These beliefs may be deeply ingrained in our everyday life. The way we act, think, and how we feel is affected by these core beliefs. Your core beliefs can be wrong, and they can be changed. Core beliefs can result in a deeply rooted need to do things perfectly and receive the approval from those around us. As a teen, these two components can result in negative beliefs that will impact you throughout your life.

Perfectionism

This negative belief forms when you feel as though you are not good enough. This type of belief can push you to better areas of your life. While wanting to improve upon things in your life is a great attribute to have, perfectionism can result in constant let downs and failures. Perfectionism can make you feel as though you are less than those around you, unworthy, or unable to accomplish what you desire.

The way you talk to yourself can help you identify if you have perfectionist beliefs. Constantly making should comments like, "I should do better in school," "I should have tried harder during practice," and "I should have said something different during class" show a perfectionist mindset. These should statement you say to yourself will make you feel as though others do not accept you or that you are not trying your best to reach your full potential.

Having a belief system of perfectionism can result in feeling alone, panic attacks, anxiety, and depression. This makes it difficult to set and move toward the goals you want to reach. Those with a perfectionist belief system will often never feel satisfied with themselves or feel that others will never accept them for who they are. You will find yourself placing more merit on your accomplishments than on your values, and therefore, your self-worth can be greatly hindered.

Need for Approval

As a teen, you want to be liked by your peers and exceed the expectations your teachers or parents have placed on you. It is normal to want to be liked and included, but the constant need for approval can lead to low self-esteem, anxiety, anger, and disappointment. When you begin to measure your self-worth by how much others like you,

you will begin to develop an overly critical inner dialog with yourself. You will jump to assumptions and run through list after list of all the things you should have said, could have done, and what ifs. This constant need for approval from others can leave you on the defensive and can, as a result, begin to push people away from you.

Not everyone is going to like you and be your friend, and most of the time, this is going to be for absolutely no reason. There is nothing wrong with that, and there is nothing wrong with the person you are. But this belief system of needing the approval of others will cause you to lose your own self-identity. You will constantly be doing things or acting a certain way because you think it is how you will get more approval from others.

How Your Beliefs Affect the Way You Think and Act

Your beliefs will affect your behavior in every situation. The way you behave will reinforce your beliefs. When we have negative beliefs about ourselves, we will feel inadequate, undeserving, and simply terrible. When we create a belief about ourselves, we often automatically take it as truth in any situation. Our beliefs are how we identify things and people as being either good or bad, whether a situation is dangerous or safe, or if our behavior is acceptable or unacceptable. They play an integral part in whether we believe our goals are achievable or not.

We can also project our core beliefs onto others. This projection is based on how we assume others view us. If you are bullied, you might begin to form the belief around what the bully says to you and begin to perceive yourself in this same way. Eventually, you will begin to think that everyone you meet will perceive in this way as well.

Beliefs are deeply rooted in all areas of our lives. We may have hundreds of beliefs that dictate our behavior, thoughts, and emotions. Our beliefs will result in having automatic thoughts about ourselves and those around us. Some of these thoughts serve us well, but many are not based on facts and can hold us back. Beliefs are connected to our subconscious mind, which is constantly looking to validate these beliefs. When we have negative or limiting beliefs, we unknowingly behave and think in a way that will further support these beliefs.

When you have negative beliefs, you ignore any evidence that opposes these beliefs and instead focus on the things that strengthen them. Our beliefs act as filters. We see what reinforces them and

neglect what opposes them. Changing our beliefs requires a focus on all the facts and not just those that feed the beliefs that are unwanted.

Identify Your Core Beliefs

Beliefs can be formed because of a number of factors. Most teens tend to develop core beliefs through their experiences and the way their caregivers treat them or act around them. For example, teens may develop a core belief about money that is negative when they constantly witness their parents stressed overpaying bills. Parents who constantly warn their children to be careful may instill in their children a core belief that the world is an unsafe place or to look at many things as a threat. Both these examples can cause children to grow into teens and then adults who are anxious.

Additional beliefs may have developed at a young age for good reason but no longer serve you well as you get older. For instance, a child that grows up in an abusive household may develop the core belief that they are powerless or that sticking up for themselves only brings about more suffering; they develop the belief that they are helpless. As the child grows and moves away from this toxic environment, this core belief no longer serves them.

When you are trying to identify your core beliefs, the first place you can turn to is your thoughts. Your thoughts can help you notice themes, and these themes can be the foundation for your core beliefs. Ask yourself some of the following questions to identify your core beliefs.

- What events in your life may contribute to your beliefs?

- What is your family dynamic like?

- What lessons did you learn from an early age?

- How have or do these lessons affect the way you see the world around you, the people you encounter, and the way you view yourself?

Changing Negative Beliefs

For many, our beliefs are formed by simply believing what is told to us. Since at a young age, we are unable to understand whether something is fact or opinion, we simply go along with what we are told. These negative beliefs can result in developing anxiety, phobias, anger issues, and being shy.

- Negative beliefs and anxiety - The negative beliefs that are attached to anxiety are often one of the weaknesses. When we strive to be perfect, we can feel a great deal of disappointment with ourselves and from others. We can place too much pressure on ourselves and place a significant amount of importance on meeting other people's expectations. This can lead to thoughts and fear of failure and what others may think of you. This in return triggers an enormous amount of anxiety.

- Negative beliefs and phobias - Fear makes us behave and thing in highly negative ways. An extreme fear of people. places or things cause use to develop phobias around those factors. Phobias are often an irrational fear. We may have no real reason to be afraid but have strengthened this fear through our thinking and actions so that we feel paralyzed when confronting these phobias.

- Negative beliefs and anger - Irrational anger is destructive and enables us to think clearly. This will often result in destructive

behavior. Extreme anger can result in chronic stress and can also transform into depression. When we are unable to manage our anger, properly express our anger, or control our impulses when frustrated, we do or say things we regret. Beliefs that form around anger are often a result of trauma or negative experiences that we never took the time to reevaluate or talk through.

- Negative beliefs and shyness - Shyness can often develop out of fear. You might formulate the belief that you act awkward in social settings because you heard over and over that you are just shy. In reality, you may have never noticed that your behavior could be taken negatively and instead of trying to change your behavior in social settings, it was justified. You may not be shy at all, but it becomes your default response when you don't talk as much or interact when around others. Simply having this belief could be the whole reason why you don't speak up more.

Negative core beliefs impact our thoughts, feelings, and behaviors, and changing them will take time and persistence. To rid ourselves of these negative beliefs, there has to be a new positive belief that replaces them, and a new way of thinking needs to be implemented to support these new beliefs.

To create new positive beliefs, you will need to learn to anticipate when the negative beliefs arise. There are countless situations in your day that will trigger limiting beliefs to arise, and each situation will cause you to respond and cycle through negative thoughts. Begin to record when these negative beliefs arise and the thoughts that follow.

When you want to change your core beliefs, you must first identify what those beliefs are. Think about all the areas of your life; which areas do you want to see an improvement in? Consider how you might have attempted to improve these areas before. What thoughts surround how you feel about your efforts in improving these areas? What behaviors do you notice when you are confronting these areas of your life? Are there areas of your life you are not happy about or that you don't feel fully connect or committed to? Are there areas of your life that make you feel inadequate, powerless, or held back?

Once you are able to answer these questions, you can begin to log your day. Creating a log can help you identify when your thoughts, behaviors, or emotions are motivated by a negative belief. You can then begin to rephrase the thoughts you have around the belief and transform it into one that is more positive.

Create a log

Situation: When did the negative occur. Who were you with? What were you doing?

Belief: What was the negative belief?

Negative Thoughts: What thoughts occurred when you noticed this belief?

New Positive Belief: What is a more empowering belief you can have in this situation?

Realistic thoughts: What evidence do you have that supports this new positive belief?

Create a log like this every time you find yourself stuck on a negative belief.

Determination and Commitment

Determination is necessary if you are going to overcome any hardship in life. You will need to determine when things become uncomfortable or when you face challenges that bring on an overwhelming number of negative thoughts and emotions. Without determination, you will never be able to follow through on the commitments you make with yourself or to the goals you want to achieve.

If you want to be able to overcome your fears, anxiety, depression, negative thinking, or destructive behavior, you need to be committed to the process. Completing the exercises in this book is proof of that commitment. Implementing the tips, techniques, and tools outlined in the following pages will take determination. Trying once and not getting the desired result will not allow you to see the changes you want. Utilizing these CBT guides will allow you to fully understand all the potential you possess and will allow you to reach that potential.

Fully understanding how your thoughts, behaviors, and emotions all affect one another will allow you to better determine and commit to the changes you seek. Focusing on each of these areas and being honest with yourself is the most effective way to produce change. Not only will these changes immediately benefit you as you navigate your teenage years, but they will benefit you even more as you move into adulthood.

Exercises

Rethinking Your Thoughts

You can notice your negative core beliefs easily if they tend to be an all-or-nothing phrase. Meaning you have the same belief no matter what situation you are in. When you have these beliefs, there are a number of questions you can ask yourself and steps you can take that will help you reword the negative beliefs. Below, you will find some of the most common negative beliefs as well as exercises you should complete if you have these negative beliefs. Go through each one and feel free to add your own negative beliefs and what you can do to counter them when they arise.

I am worthless.

- **Create a list of at least five qualities that make you unique.**

1.

2.

3.

4.

5.

- **Write three things you did today that helped others.**

1.

2.

3.

- **Write the names of three people who care about you.**

1.

2.

3.

- **Reevaluate the situation where this belief came about. What triggered this belief?**

•   **Identify one fact about the situation that opposes this belief.**

I am always wrong.

- **What is one subject in school that you excel in?**

- **Give three examples where you could have made a poor choice but instead choose to do the right thing.**

1.

2.

3.

- Reevaluate the situation where this belief came about. What triggered this belief?

- **Identify one fact about the situation that opposes this belief.**

- **List three times when you felt proud of yourself.**

1.

2.

3.

- List three times when you answered a question correctly.

1.

2.

3.

- Give an example of when you made your parents, teachers, or friends proud.

- Reevaluate the situation where this belief came about. What triggered this belief?

- Identify one fact about the situation that opposes this belief.

- Reevaluate the situation where this belief came about. What triggered this belief?

- **Identify one fact about the situation that opposes this belief.**

- **List the names of three of your closest friends.**

1.

2.

3.

- **List all the family members you see regularly.**

1.

2.

3.

4.

5.

- Reevaluate the situation where this belief came about. What triggered this belief?

- Identify one fact about the situation that opposes this belief.

- Reevaluate the situation where this belief came about. What triggered this belief?

- Identify one fact about the situation that opposes this belief.

- Reevaluate the situation where this belief came about. What triggered this belief?

- Identify one fact about the situation that opposes this belief.

NEGATIVE BELIEF   NEW BELIEF

- I AM WORTHLESS; I AM PROUD OF WHO I AM
- I AM ALWAYS WRONG; I AM ALWAYS LEARNING SOMETHING NEW
- I CAN'T DO ANYTHING RIGH; I CAN DO A LOT OF THINGS
- I AM UNWANTED; I AM LOVED
- NOBODY LIKES ME; I AM SURROUNDED BY PEOPLE WHO LOVE ME
- I AM STUPID; I AM ABLE TO LEARN WHAT I DON'T KNOW
- I ALWAYS GET LEFT OUT; I AM FUN TO BE AROUND
- I AM NOT GOOD AT ANYTHING; I AM CAPABLE OF ANYTHING

Defining the Objective

Now that you have identified the areas of life you want to improve in the previous chapter and understand how your beliefs impact the way you think, feel, and behave, you can create a goal to work toward.

- Identify one area of life you want to improve.

- List the negative beliefs you have toward this area of life.

- Create new positive beliefs that will help you work toward improving this area.

- List three things you can do that will improve this area.

- What would making these changes mean?

NEGATIVE BELIEF:

NEW BELIEF:

GOAL 1:

WHY IS THIS IMPORTANT TO YOU?

ACTION   1.

STEP   2.

3.

Chapter 4: Values

Values are the guiding post that will help you become the person you want to become. Values will help you set and achieve goals that will allow you to be successful in life based on what is important to you. Values shape the relationships you have, the activities you participate in, and how you engage in the world around you.

What Are Values?

Values are established by you but can be imposed on you from an early age. Oftentimes, teenagers will adopt the values of their parents or will base their values on their upbringing. Though some may be modified as you get older to better align with who you are, they are often continuous or there is no endpoint. Values are not goals they are linked directly to who you are as a person, what you enjoy, and what matters most to you. When we do not recognize our own true values and only live our life according to the values we have aligned with based on our childhood, we can live an entire life that is not the life we had wanted.

Values can be big and small. They are personal to each person uniquely. For each area of your life, you may have one or many core values. To identify your own unique values, you will need to look at a number of factors.

Identify Your Values

First, how you were raised affects your values. Consider the values you identify with that are because of how you were raised (be respectful to your parents, follow the rules of the house). What values do your parents identify with (being viewed as educated, being viewed as hard-working)? What values are present in the way you live your life or in the way your parents live their lives (you focus on getting good grades because education is important, you remain quiet when adults are around and never voice your opinion)? What values are stressed in your family (you regularly practice a certain religion, there

is regular quality time with family such as game nights or vacations)? How were values present to you when you were facing a consequence for your behavior or actions, either as a reward or punishment (you made high honors so you got a new game system, you disagreed with what your parents told you so you got your phone taken away)?

Next, consider the things that you do. Do you play sports, do well in school, play an instrument? Why do you participate in these activities? Is it for enjoyment or to please your parents? What subjects interest you or what topics do you like to talk about with your friends or family? What can you find in this interest that led you to something you value?

Now, consider how the answers to these questions reflect how you were brought up? Are there some values that stick out that do not completely resonate with you? Are there some that you want to strengthen your connection with?

Why Are Values Important in Life?

Your values will help guide you to make the right choices in your life. When you establish your values, you can also come up with new ways to achieve the goals you set. These activities will support your values and feel more rewarding.

Values will allow you to align your behavior and thoughts in a way that helps you succeed. They will help you decide what friends you should keep, what career to pursue, how you want to be viewed by others. and what goals to set. Values are what will motivate you to pursue goals. They are not a goal of themselves but are a standard to how you want to experience the world around you. For a teen, you may not fully understand all the values you may want to adopt or know which

are the most important to you. As you get older, new values will come about that will dictate how you live your life. Below, you will find a list of some of the most common early values that you might find important.

Freedom/Independence

For a teen, freedom often reflects how responsible we think we are or how responsible our parents think we are. Every teen strives to have more freedom. They want to stay out later with friends, get a job, and be able to buy things with their own money. They want to feel as though they are capable and that their parents trust them to make good decisions.

Love

Teens need to feel loved and understand that they are capable of loving others. A teen who values receiving love and affection may align their behaviors in a way that allows them to achieve this goal. They may be more respectful, considerate, or caring toward others. However, if they often lack or are unable to appropriately understand what love is or is supposed to look like, they may find themselves valuing having loving relationships but not understand what that is really supposed to be like.

Friendship

What type of relationship do you want to form with your friends? What value would you place on having strong and meaningful friendships? How do you want to be viewed as a friend?

Loyalty

Loyalty is a reflection of trust. Not only do we want to have loyal friends but we want to be viewed as loyal ourselves. Loyalty is related to being able to trust those around you and being able to trust yourself. Loyalty is what will allow you to make commitments to yourself and others and follow through on what you say you are going to do.

Respect

Respect is connected to self-respect. To be able to respect others, we must first learn to respect ourselves in a positive way. Developing respect and self-respect is vital to having a successful relationship with peers, family, and yourself. Being able to see the value you offer to others will make it easier for you to see the value in others as well. When you treat yourself with respect, it sets a standard for how you want others to treat you as well.

Faith

Faith can mean a number of things to different people. Your faith is often the result of how you are brought up. For many teens, this value is one that is instilled in them from their parents or community. They may value faith but have no real reason as to why this may be important. Additionally, they may be limited in their options to pursue different spiritual paths. Spend some time determining what you put faith in.

Family

What types of relationships do you want to have with your parents, siblings, and other family members? How do you want your role in the family to be viewed?

Safety

Feeling safe and secure is a deeply rooted value. From birth, children have a need to feel as though they are safe and protected. When safety is not a concern, it can lead to making poor decisions, hurting others, and being unkind to yourself. Safety as a value requires you to focus on what makes you feel safe, how others make you feel safe, and what makes you feel unsafe.

Success

Success is different for everyone. As a teen, success might simply mean making the varsity team; for others, it could mean being awarded a scholarship at the most prestigious school in the country; and for some teens, success is finding joy and happiness is what they do. In general, though, success is accomplishing the goals you set for yourself through hard work, dedication, and persistence.

Health

For teens, their health may not be a major concern. They may not understand or have ever been taught the importance of maintaining good health. But it is a value you want to seriously consider. Having good health allows you to be more active in your own life. When you are healthy, you not only feel physically strong but mentally strong as well. Adopting health as a value doesn't have to mean never eating cookies and cake or running 6 miles a day. It can simply mean that you take care of the body you have mentally, physically, and emotionally to the best of your ability.

Recognition

Valuing recognition means that you not only want to ensure that others see and acknowledge your accomplishments but that you take the time to do the same for others. Recognition can help us feel good

about ourselves and can validate our hard work, but it can also lead to attaching too much importance on how others view you.

Popularity

For many teens, popularity is a high priority on their value list. Being popular often means you are less likely to be bullied, will receive special treatment, and experience a boost your self-esteem. Popularity, however, does not play a vital role once you enter into your adult years. Being popular may be a value while in high school, but developing your own self-worth, self-respect, and self-esteem that will carry on after high school and help you succeed in life may be more important.

Free Time

Teens have a lot on their plate, and a majority of their time is spent in school and completing schoolwork. Add in household responsibilities, extracurricular activities, and a job, and many are left with very little free time. Placing free time as a top value can help teens understand how to balance all the daily demands of life and responsibilities with things they enjoy doing and time to rest and relax.

Gratitude

Gratitude is a powerful and effective way to bring more happiness into your life. From a young age, children and teens who are able to show and be more grateful for what they have tend to be happier and more successful. Gratitude is the act of being thankful and aware of the things you do have. You can be grateful for what you have and still work hard to obtain the things you want but when you do not succeed or get what you wish for, you are less likely to be devastated by the outcomes or length of time it takes to obtain what you are working for.

Happiness

Happiness is connected to a number of areas in your life. Happiness is not just a feeling or emotion but can also be a way of living. Those who value their own happiness and the happiness of others tend to feel as though they belong or are accepted. Happiness is a choice that one makes. Choosing happiness as a core value will help guide you through making tough decisions. It will also remind you to stay true to yourself and can boost your self-worth.

When you know the values you hold, you can better make the necessary adjustments to your thoughts, emotions, and behavior to align with these values. Your values will play a vital role in your success in overcoming obstacles in your life. These values will help guide you in making the best choices and will assure that the choice you make will benefit you.

How Do Our Values Influence Our Choices and Behaviors?

Your personal values will be what can guide you through difficult choices. When you have identified your values, your behaviors will align with what supports those values. How you show up, the relationships you build, and the effort you put into school and work will all reflect on your values. Values can be used to ensure that your behavior or response to challenging situations is how you should be behaving based on who you are and who you want to be.

Moral Dilemmas

Teens are confronted with moral dilemmas frequently through the young adult years. These circumstances are what will help develop and be able to regulate their emotional and behavioral responses in a variety of situations. These moral dilemmas will allow teens to cope and work through social influences. When they have clearly identified their core values, teens are able to more easily work through these uncomfortable moments. When they have not identified their values, teens can suffer from anxiety and depression.

Understanding the Values of Our Life

Values are a way of understanding who you are and who you want to be. When you identify your values, you can use them as a way to stay centered and happy no matter what situations you may be confronted with. Your values can help you understand why you do things the way

you do, whether in how you behave, think, or approach certain situations.

Values are not just a guideline for how we behave or act; they can also inspire us to work through problems. Your values will reflect what is most important to you.

When you are clear about what is important to you, then you will be able to make choices and behave in alignment with these values. Teens are faced with a variety of situations where having clear values will help them make the best choice, such as drinking and driving, join their friends when they make fun of the new student, or neglecting homework to play video games. Values can be reviewed and addressed for big and small decisions.

How Values Guide Us

Values guide us by reminding us what is important to us. In each situation, you face you can simply ask what is more important to you. You will make the choice that best aligns with your values. When trying to make a choice between two options, being reminded of the person you are and the person you want to become will make the choice much easier.

Exercise

The Pyramid of Your Values

Choose 5 values and list them in order of importance. You can do this easily by thinking of them on a pyramid. The most important value will go at the top.

When ranking your values, take into consideration the ones you want to be working toward first. The values you rank here will be a reference as you work through your challenging thoughts and behaviors. They will allow you to set specific goals that you can begin working toward achieving using the information throughout this book.

Once you have listed your values, consider what core beliefs you have and what areas of life these values fall into. Are there thoughts, emotions, or behaviors that you exhibit that do not align with these values? List them out.

Chapter 5: Conquer Negative Thinking

Thoughts are meant to come and go. When we get stuck on certain thoughts, we can end up acting out in unfavorable ways. Negative thinking that you allow to consume your day can lead you to make decisions that have severe consequences. Learning how to acknowledge these thoughts, see them as they are, and allow them to flow away from you will allow you to have more control over all areas of your life.

How Do Negative Thoughts Arise?

Thoughts are one of the key components of CBT. We have millions of thoughts throughout the day, and most go unnoticed but have a significant amount of influence on our actions and behaviors without us even realizing it. Some thoughts leave you running in circles, lower your self-esteem, and keep you from remaining in the present moment.

Thoughts can flow through your mind as a simple word, a phrase, or an image. Some of these can be difficult to ignore or move through your thought process and feel as though they are just stuck in your head. This can lead to what is referred to as ruminating. This is excessive worry or focusing on things that can go wrong in the future. These thoughts are often unhelpful and can even be harmful.

Though it may feel as though some of these thoughts are stuck in your mind like superglue, thoughts are just the chatter that takes place in your head. Most of these thoughts have no significant meaning. They are often just a replay of events that have or may occur. Though they feel as though they can consume you, you can learn what chatter you tune into. You can learn to watch your thoughts just as they are, chatter. You can learn to tune out the negative chatter and turn up the positive thoughts.

When you learn to catch the negative thoughts you can learn to decipher the misleading assumptions that are connected to them. Negative thoughts can cause us to make careless mistakes, harm ourselves or others, and can cause problems with family, friends, and at school.

Our thoughts affect our behavior in a number of ways. Do you forgive or retaliate, withdraw or engage, give up or persevere? Your thoughts will either help you alleviate the stress and challenges you face or they can cause you to prolong and find it more difficult to get over some obstacles.

Negative Automatic Thoughts

Negative automatic thoughts are considered a cognitive distortion. These thought patterns are often the result of constantly using "I should" statements. Individuals who suffer from anxiety and depression will have many more negative automatic thoughts. We often feel as though we have no control over negative automatic thoughts. These thoughts are triggered by certain cues and can tear us down. But, these negative thoughts can be used to help build us up, and they can be used to work in our favor to be more successful. When these thoughts tear us down, we suffer from more anxiety.

What Feeds Our Negative Thoughts?

When a negative thought occurs, there tends to be a snowball effect that happens. One negative thought can cause another, then another, and another. The more we are focused on the negative thoughts, the stronger they grow. Our behaviors, emotions, and thoughts all feed into negative thinking patterns. We develop habits that make us feel as though it is perfectly normal to constantly fight off or cycle through negative thoughts. In reality, negative thoughts occur more often once you get into the habit of giving them so much attention.

Emotions play an integral role in negative thinking. Many times, we may not understand where our negative thoughts are coming from, but we may notice a change in our body such as feeling more tense or nauseous. These are clear signs that your negative thoughts are occurring because of unrecognized emotions. Once we do recognize the emotion, more negative thoughts form. Emotions, however, can be simply accepted and then let go. Once they run their course, you can shift to more positive feelings. If you focus on the negative thoughts that are occurring at the same time as the emotion, it is more likely that this will prolong the emotional reaction you are having.

When we are out of tune with ourselves and our bodies, this can fuel negative thinking as well. Those who are more self-aware tend to have more positive thoughts. Those who lack understanding in themselves will often find it more difficult to redirect negative thoughts or even spot the negativity before it has spiraled out of control.

How Negative Thinking Affects Our Lives

Our negative thoughts can make us believe in the false assumptions we may form about ourselves, others, and the world around us. Though these thoughts have no truth to them, you can easily jump to a conclusion when a negative thought enters your mind.

Negative thoughts can take us away from the present moment. When a negative thought arises, we automatically tune in, out of habit. Then we get sucked into the negative spiral and miss out on enjoying what we are actually doing. Negative thoughts can also make us want to avoid situations we know will trigger the negativity.

Additionally, negative thoughts can make us more prone to a number of mental health issues such as anxiety and depression. Negative thoughts cause us to go into high alert as they often signal the brain and the body that something is wrong, even if there is no real threat.

When confronting problems, negative thoughts make it more difficult for us to find solutions or work through the problem. For teens, negative thinking not only makes it more challenging for them to address their problems, but it makes it more likely for them to make a choice the results in negative consequences.

Negative thoughts affect how we think about ourselves, others, and the world around us. When you have negative thoughts, you may automatically make negative assumptions, and your behaviors will align in this same negative manner. Identifying not only your negative thoughts but your negative thought patterns can help you make major improvements in multiple areas of your life.

Five Negative Thinking Habits

Negative thinking habits can be easier to stop once you are able to identify which patterns they fall into. Below, you will learn about the most common thinking patterns that you may struggle with.

"I Can't" Habit

This negative thought pattern constantly has you focusing on what you are lacking. "I can't" thoughts arise when you face new encounters or difficult situations. When these thoughts occur, they can lead to feeling anxious or sad. You may feel as though you can't make new friends, you can't pass your math test, or that you can't do anything right. The "I can't" negative thought process is most often due to focus on past failures or on beliefs that others have imposed on you.

"All or Nothing" Habit

All-or-nothing thinking is also known as black-or-white thinking. This thinking involves only seeing the extreme results, which can be one way or the other where there is no gray area. This type of thinking is common for those focused on being a perfectionist, or those that always perceiving themselves as a failure when they do not meet their own expectations.

A few examples of this type of thinking could be:

- Thinking you failed a test just because you do not get a 100%.
- Always thinking nothing good ever happens to you just because one thing in your day goes wrong.
- The people around you are either your best friend or your worst enemy.

When you suffer from this type of thinking, you never see the middle ground. To change this type of thinking, you need to catch these extreme "one side or the other" thoughts and counter them with alternative thoughts that are supported by facts.

When you are constantly in the all-or-nothing thought pattern, you may find that you catastrophize things, only see the negatives in the situation, or may blame yourself for problems that have nothing to do with you. When you think in this extreme manner, you quickly lower your self-esteem and begin to take responsibility for issues in other people's lives that you had nothing to with. These thoughts will often arise as a simple negative and quickly spiral out of control, especially when you do not stop to consider all the facts or the lack thereof.

Exercise

Can you think of a time when you had all-or-nothing thoughts? List three of them now.

1.

2.

3.

Now, list three alternative thoughts that oppose these thoughts. These new thoughts should be somewhere along the middle ground of the

extreme spectrum.

1.

2.

3.

"I Should, You Should" Habit

When you have the habit of thinking in the "I should, you should" thought pattern, you most likely are applying strict rules to yourself and others. When you have this type of thought pattern, you run into the challenge of not being able to be flexible with others and therefore always feel let down. The "I should, you should" way of thinking often fuels feelings of guilt; you might focus on what you should have done in a certain situation or what someone else should have done.

This thought pattern can also make it more difficult for you to identify or acknowledge that there are things you may not actually know. You might see this thought pattern occur frequently when you need to do a group project, when you are at work, or even when you are just trying to decide where to hang out with your friends.

Getting stuck in the "I should, you should" thought pattern can lead to ruminating over your experiences. You may spend an exuberant amount of time overthinking how you performed on a test, what you said to your crush, or what someone else said to you early in the day. When we get stuck ruminating on the events that occurred, we will feel more anxious, frustrated, disappointed, and stressed.

"It's Not Fair" Habit

The "it's not fair" thinking habit can be a common negative thought pattern for many teens. You may feel as if you were completely deserving of an A or that it is not your fault a certain event occurred. You will blame others for your own failures and never actually analyze the situation to find out what went wrong, so you are unable to make improvements within yourself.

This negative thought pattern does not allow you to grow and be successful. Since you never address what you could have done differently, you never know how to improve. When you get stuck in this pattern, you will often avoid taking chances and never fully apply yourself so that you can live up to your full potential, and this can lead to depression and anxiety.

"Mind Reading" Habit

Those who adopt a mind-reading thought process tends to be 100% certain of what others are thinking with or without facts to support these thoughts. This results in constantly making assumptions about others and always thinking you know what the other person thinks and wants.

Prime examples of mind reading include:

- When someone does not say "Hi" to you, you immediately think they hate you.

- When your friend doesn't respond back quickly after you send them a message, you begin to think they are mad at you and you begin to think of all the reasons they could be mad at you.

When you catch yourself stuck in this mind-reading habit, you need to look at things from the other person's perspective. Look at the situation in which this negative thought arises and consider the facts that are observable from the other person's point of view, not just yours. Once you have filtered through the facts, you need to remind yourself that there is no way for you to know what the other person is thinking, and you have no idea what may have happened before you encountered this person.

Exercise

Think of times when you have gotten stuck in a mind-reading habit and write three examples now.

1.

2.

3.

Now write three new thoughts that will help you remember that unless they have told you, you have no idea if there is proof in these thoughts.

1.

2.

3.

Eliminating Negative Thoughts

You can begin to identify these negative ways of thinking by becoming aware of how these thoughts can affect you. Some cues that you are stuck in a negative thought pattern include:

1.	You feel a sudden onset of negative emotions such as anxiety or resentment. When you feel a sudden shift in your emotions, you are most likely dealing with a negative thought.

2.	You can't seem to get yourself out of a negative mood. These moods are often fueled by negative thoughts. If you notice that you are irritable during the day for no apparent reason or you feel dread throughout the day, these are clues that you are battling with negative thoughts.

3.	Your behavior is not aligning with the goals or values you have identified. When you catch yourself not doing the things you know you should be doing or want to be doing but cannot seem to get yourself to follow through, this is due to negative thoughts.

Negative thoughts can be eliminated using a number of techniques. The first step with any of them is to be able to recognize the negative thoughts and the mind trick you play out when these thoughts occur. To do this, you need to take note of the thoughts that occur in between what happens to you and your response to that event. This is the time period, which is brief, where the negative thoughts will arise and cause you to have behaviors that are unwanted or emotions that are unnecessary. Once you are able to devalue these thoughts, you can create an alternative way of thinking that is based on facts and not just assumptions.

When you get into the habit of being able to identify the negative thinking habits you encounter and write them out, along with an alternative thought, you will begin to realize how inaccurate your thoughts are. After going through this process a few times, you may see these negative thoughts occur less or that you are able to easily debunk them with an alternative thought. Compare your negative thoughts to reality. We feed into our negative thoughts because we do not question how unreasonable or inaccurate they are. When you notice you are having a negative thought, you want to reflect on what has actually occurred without making assumptions. Before you begin to feed into the negative thoughts and reinforce them with behaviors, look for evidence and the supporting facts of the situation.

Hypothesizing

Some thoughts, however, may keep you stuck. No matter how much you believe in the alternative thought you create, the original one continues to show up. It may take a handful of times for you to remind yourself of the alternative thought, and even then, the original thought continues to consume you.

When this occurs, there are additional techniques you can use to help move past the negative thinking habit.

One way to counter strong-willed negative thoughts is to test them out. Just as you would test out a hypothesis in a science experiment, you may need to test out your negative thoughts along with the alternative to gather supporting evidence. To accomplish this, you will need to recognize the negative thought, then list the evidence you have both for and against this thought. Once you have your lists, you can look through them and create a new hypothesis or thought that will allow you to move past the negative thought.

Visualization

Allowing thoughts to simply pass through your mind without letting them reel you in is the first step to overcoming your negative thinking. Visualization can assist you in letting your thoughts simply pass through. One way to utilize this technique is to imagine the thoughts that flow through your mind as a cloud. Picture yourself laying under a blue sky in a wide-open field. You see a large, white, cloud begin to drift across the sky. You lay back and watch as it glides across the sky. It may morph into different shapes and take on different forms but, you remain lying on the ground. You watch as it slowly crawls out of sight.

Just as you watch the cloud pass across the sky, you can watch your thoughts pass through your head. As you watched the cloud, you did not get up and begin to drift along under it or with it. You simply let it go in the direction it was going. You can learn to master this skill when it comes to the negative thoughts you approach each day.

Exercises

Focus on Your Strengths

Begin to get into the habit of ending your day by remembering the good that occurred. Each night, write down at least three things that happened in your day that went well. Also, write why these things went well. Completing this exercise each night will support more positive thoughts and can help you shift into having more positive beliefs.

Reframe Your Thoughts

Reframing your thoughts can help you see things from a different perspective, which can have an impact on unwanted behaviors. Exercises to reframe your thoughts include:

1. List the advantages and disadvantages of having the thought and then evaluate the list. You will notice that some

of the thoughts are helpful, and others will not align with the goals you have set.

2. List all the possibilities of a situation and then assign them a percentage to how likely it is that one of those other possibilities is actually true as opposed to the way you think about the situation.

Question Your Thoughts

1. What is an alternative outcome that is possible aside from the one you are worried about?

2. Are your emotions clouding your judgment (are your feelings making you feel more strongly about the thought, which is causing you to believe it is true)?

2. What has occurred in a similar situation in the past?

4. How did you get through this situation in the past or what was the outcome?

5. How likely is it that your thoughts are actually true?

6. What is really the worst thing that could happen in this situation?

7. If the worst-case scenario does occur, how would you cope with it?

8. What is another way you can look at this situation?

9. Are you able to predict the future?

Chapter 6: Conquer Anxiety

Worry and anxiety are very similar ways you respond to uncomfortable or new situations. Both worry and anxiety can lead you to act out on irrational thoughts. When you worry, you are constantly thinking about the future. You are unsure of what is about to about or will happen. This is typical when you are concerned about passing a test or if you will find a prom date. This type of worry becomes justified by the thoughts that follow the feelings. Thoughts of having to skip prom, failing a class, having to take summer classes, or miss out on the Friday night game, and a long list of other what ifs, can overwhelm your mind. This leads to an inability to concentrate or remain in the present moment. Worry is a normal characteristic of anxiety. It is normal to worry. It becomes a concern when you are so worried and concerned about the "what ifs" that you are restless.

What Is Anxiety?

Anxiety is the way your body responds to stress. When you are confronted with something you fear or makes you tense, your body and thoughts will mimic the situation. This can result in freezing, trying to get away from what you are encountering, or going into a panic. This anxiety triggers the body's naturally fight or flight response. Anxiety forces us to focus on an imagined threat, which causes feelings of fear or nervousness. These feelings result in behaviors that help us avoid the fear outcome.

You can become physically affected by anxiety. You may feel more aches, pains, headaches, and digestive issues. It can interfere with your sleep, cause you to grind your teeth unintentionally, and can make it difficult to breathe at times. These physical issues can manifest in behavioral issues such as going out of your way to avoid people or places. You may find yourself consumed by a topic or feel the need to spend extra time focusing on finding a solution. You may find yourself so hyper-focused on something that you lose track of time. These behaviors can escalate and turn into more serious issues, like skipping school, intentionally not turning in assignments, no longer participating in extracurricular activities, or not socializing with others altogether.

Though it is natural and even healthy to feel anxious from time to time, when this anxiety becomes overwhelming, lasts for extended periods of time, or comes about with no known triggers, this can turn into a serious anxiety disorder. This extreme type of anxiety can significantly hinder your quality of life and can interfere with your daily routines.

Having an anxiety disorder seems like a never-ending battle with your irrational thoughts. Even recognizing your thoughts still doesn't take away the fear and overwhelming sensation. Through deliberate action and clear understanding, you can begin to conquer your anxiety and shift your mindset to one that is more empowering. Anxiety can be used to motivate us and focus on the things that matter most to us.

Where Does Anxiety Come From?

Anxiety can make us feel as though we have no control over ourselves or our surroundings. Though anxiety is a normal and healthy reaction to a situation we are not used to, this can develop into an anxiety disorder that can spiral out of control.

While factors like physical health, hormone balance, and chemicals released by the body impact how you respond to anxiety, a number of other factors play a more significant role. For many, anxiety causes the same reactions to a situation as fear does. The major difference between the two is that people often understand what they are afraid of when they have feelings of fear; with anxiety, it can often be more difficult to understand what the trigger is.

The most common reasons people will feel anxious include:

- Peer or social pressure
- School or work-related pressure
- Family strain
- Health issues
- Substance abuse

When you become anxious you may feel:

- Shaky
- Nauseous
- Stomach discomfort
- Muscle tension
- Headache
- Back pain
- Irregular heartbeat
- Flushed in the face
- Tingling of the hands, arms, or legs

For most individuals, these symptoms of anxiety come and go without much interference. For others, it can be debilitating and cause extreme fears that have no logical explanation. This leads them to avoid what they believe are the triggers for their symptoms. These avoidances can begin small, simply avoiding certain peer circles, and then evolve into more serious issues where an individual may avoid all social settings and isolate themselves.

How Does Anxiety Manifest?

Anxiety disorders are often the result of a number of factors. Life events, genetics, biochemical factors, and personality all have an impact on the development of anxiety disorders. The precise circumstances and triggers are often unidentified until the individual is carefully observed. Only through observation and mindfulness can one begin to understand the true triggers for their anxiety. Anxiety manifests when we imagine there is a threat that may or may not actually occur, and it is fueled through thinking and behaviors.

There are four common features that anxiety will present.

1. There is often an unidentified or unknown debilitating fear. This fear interferes with performing daily tasks and can make it feel impossible to enjoy life.

2. The anxiety the individual feels is often confusing. Because there is no known cause for what is making the individual feel anxious, it can become frustrating and challenging to address or talk about.

3. Even when a logical explanation for the anxiety is identified, there will often be no decrease in symptoms.

4.   No matter what type of anxiety disorder you suffer from, understand there is a way to cope, reduce, and even eliminate the anxiety you are suffering from.

Number four is key to remember. Though you may feel trapped by your anxiety now, there are ways you can manage and even eliminate it from your life.

How Does Anxiety Affect Us?

An individual who is able to manage their anxiety can use it to help work through difficult times and avoid dangerous situations. It also helps the individual think more clearly about the situation. When faced with anxiety on a regular basis multiple times throughout the day, it can have the opposite effect. Anxiety that occurs for no reason and causes you to feel panicked or afraid most of the day is a serious concern.

Anxiety can have serious effects on your health. The first and most common symptom that an anxiety disorder is present is when you suffer from digestive issues. You may have frequent stomach pains or

cramps, lose your appetite daily, and have irregular bowel movements. These issues can worsen over time and weaken the immune system.

Anxiety causes the body to remain in a constant fight or flight mode. When this occurs, the nervous system is working excessively to keep you out of harm's way. While the fight or flight response is necessary when you're actually in a dangerous situation, anxiety causes this state to be on high alert all the time. This can lead to difficulty sleeping, muscle tension, frequent headaches, and constant shifts in your mood.

Being in a constant state of anxiety forces the heart to work overtime as well. When your body is in a constant stressed and anxious state, the heart is pumping more blood and beating faster. This increase in blood pressure can cause excessive strain on the blood vessels.

The most notable way that anxiety can have a negative effect on you is over your quality of life. Living with an anxiety disorder will often limit your ability to socialize, work, focus, and enjoy the things you once loved to do. Anxiety can lead you to feel like a prisoner. Your relationships, both with family and friends, become strained. Many who suffer from anxiety disorders will often avoid meeting new people and will often stop putting effort into the friendships that they have. This only causes the anxiety to worsen and other conditions like depression to develop.

Types of Anxiety

Anxiety is not a one-size-fits-all issue. There are a number of anxiety disorders and anxiety issues that you may be suffering from.

Generalized Anxiety Disorder (GAD)

This type of anxiety causes an excessive amount of worry or fear that continues throughout the day. There is often no specific trigger to bring on the worry or fear, and when it begins, it carries over from one situation to the next.

Phobias

This is a type of anxiety that arises out of fear. Phobias are specific and can revolve around objects, events, or situations. Some of the most common phobias include fear of public speaking, fear of small spaces, fear of wide-open spaces, and fear of spiders.

Shyness

Shyness can transform into a form of social anxiety. While everyone experiences moments of shyness, it can paralyze some teens. Being shy can make it more difficult for teens to interact with their peers and can cause negative thoughts to run rampant through their minds. Shyness can impair your social experiences and cause you to withdraw when confronted with social settings.

For many, being shy is just a part of their personality, and there is nothing wrong with getting a little flushed, shaky, or nervous around

others. Feelings of discomfort are a part of healthy social development, and many children will experience these discomforts early on when their trusted caregivers are not by their side. Many children will also experience bouts of shyness when their trusted caregiver is in sight but they are around new or unfamiliar adults. Those who are shy will:

- Be unable to make eye contact when meeting someone new.
- Not speak when they meet someone new.
- Be unwilling to interact with other children they do not know.
- Withdraw and play by themselves.

These behaviors are typical for children when they are placed in unfamiliar situations or when meeting new people. This is a defense mechanism and is completely normal for children still developing their social skills. They will often grow out of these behaviors and will become more comfortable and confident when they face new people and situations.

For some children, getting over these discomforts is more challenging, and shyness can instead strengthen as they grow older instead of diminishing. Other children may have shyness as a fixed component of their personality. These children will often:

- Be struck with anxiety when in social settings.
- Be unable to interact appropriately in social settings.
- Display reserved behaviors in social settings.
- Be overall nervous around others.
- Fear being judged by others.

When shyness is a personality trait, it may not hinder your ability to connect with others. You can still make friends and will be able to

excel socially despite the discomfort. These behaviors are concerning when they begin to affect your ability to socialize and disrupt your ability to learn in the classroom. Typical signs of shyness can be an indication of social anxiety disorder. The two may be very similar, but as you will learn, social anxiety disorder hinders teens to a much greater degree than just being shy.

Social Anxiety - As we just discussed, shyness can increase as a child enters their teen years. When this occurs, the teen may be paralyzed when in new or even familiar social settings, resulting in a more serious mental block like social anxiety. Many teens suffer from some form of social anxiety. This type of anxiety is triggered in social settings such as:

- Talking in class.
- Having to give a presentation in class.

- Talking with a group of peers.
- Eating in front of others.
- Attending a party.
- Attending a school function, such as assemblies.
- Having a confrontation with someone else.
- Having attention being directed to them.
- Meeting someone new.

Those with social anxiety are afraid they will do something embarrassing and not only have a negative view of themselves but project the view they have of themselves on how others view them. These fears can keep them from participating in activities that they would find a lot of joy in doing, like playing a sport, joining an after- school club, or participating in group projects.

What makes social anxiety hard to overcome is that the fear we have seems completely logical, and it is hard to discredit because it is based on what we think or how we believe others are viewing us. But since there is no way to know what someone else is actually thinking, that leaves us feeling uneasy and uncertain. Many teens cope with this anxiety by simply avoiding what they know will trigger feelings of discomfort and uneasiness.

How to Eliminate Anxiety

When confronting anxiety, you want to disrupt the negative feedback loop that plays out in your mind. This loop begins when your anxiety is at its lowest effect, but our fear begins to generate additional thoughts that increase the anxiety. When you notice you are beginning to become fearful in a situation, stop and count to ten. This will give you a moment to pause before reacting to your fear. Take a few deep breaths and focus on the facts of the situation. Are you in any real danger? Is anyone else in any real danger? What facts of the situation can you use to contour your negative thoughts revolving around the situation?

Anxiety is not dangerous, and no harm comes from feeling anxious. Though it is uncomfortable, the first thing you can tell yourself when you are feeling anxious is that no harm will come to you. Just because you are feeling an excessive amount of fear does not mean that you are in danger, though that is exactly the way your thoughts and body is responding to this big emotion. Remind yourself that an anxiety disorder is based on unrealistic fears.

Allow yourself to confront what you fear. When you are exposed to the triggers for your anxiety, you begin to face them head-on. When you confront your anxiety through exposure, you begin to train your nervous system not to overreact. You build your confidence and strengthen your ability to confront these fears. By regularly exposing yourself to your fear, you become more aware and understanding that your anxiety cannot harm you.

For Parents

Parents, you can help alleviate some anxiety associated with shyness and social settings by reminding your teen of their positive qualities. This will allow them to recognize these qualities and can be the first step for them to feel more comfortable and confident in social settings.

Another way parents can help their anxious teens in social settings is by helping their children understand that being nervous in social settings is completely normal. By normalizing socialization, your teen will feel less alone. Discuss times when you have been nervous meeting new people either as a teen or even as an adult. Talk to them about how it made you feel nervous and shy and what you said to yourself to help you combat these uncomfortable feelings. When your teen recognizes that what they are feeling is normal and nothing to be afraid of, they can build more confidence when they enter social settings.

Exercises

Breathing Exercises

Deep breathing is a technique you can use if you are facing a situation that makes you feel anxious and is also great to practice on a daily basis to reduce stress. Deep breathing exercises are easy to do and can help you reduce feelings of anxiety immediately. When you begin to feel fear or anxious, take a deep breath in through your nose for a count of five, then exhale slowly for a count of five through your mouth. Repeat this three times, and you will feel that your body relaxes, your thoughts slow, and you are able to realistically evaluate your situation.

Meditation

Meditation allows you to focus on your thoughts, it can help you train yourself to acknowledge your thoughts and then simply let them go. Meditation for just five minutes a day can help reduce stress, anxiety, and depression.

Begin by sitting in a comfortable position (you can also do this standing). Allow your thoughts to come. When they do come, simply acknowledge them but then let them go. If you find yourself getting stuck on an unpleasant thought or feeling, it can be beneficial to repeat a reassuring phrase to yourself so that you can bring your focus back to the positive, such as "I am safe," or "I am in control," As you get into the habit of meditating, you can add different techniques, like mindfulness.

When you practice mindfulness meditation, you stay in the present moment. Pick something in your environment to focus on; this can be something visual, something you smell, or something you hear. Keep your focus on that object, and when you find your thoughts wandering elsewhere, use that thing to bring you back to the present moment.

Chapter 7: Managing Your Emotions and Moods

Moods and emotions are often used interchangeably, but they have distinct differences. Whereas emotions are experienced frequently and change regularly throughout the day, moods can have a longer-lasting effect. Your mood can affect your daily life, behavior, and thought process.

What Are Moods?

Moods are long-lasting emotional feelings. Moods can feel like phases or stages we go through. They often last a few days at a time but can last for what feels like months with no relief. External circumstances are common triggers for a shift in moods.

It is possible to feel different emotions while you are in a certain mood. You can still feel moments of happiness and joy even if you are in a sad or bad mood. Moods can arise from being overwhelmed by intense emotions that we are unsure of how to manage.

How Our Moods Influence Our Choices and Life

When we are in a certain mood, the way we approach others and the situation will vary. For instance, if you are in an ill or bad mood and you are about to meet someone new, you most likely are not going to be very receptive or optimistic about forming a new friendship with that person. Your behavior will reflect your mood.

Important Moods

There are a number of emotions and moods you will filter through daily. They can come and go, or they can make you feel stuck and out of control. Some of the most common moods you will face and learn to manage include:

- Fear - Fear can cause you to become tense and prevent you from living your life the way you want to be living it. Fear can quickly turn into anxiety when we don't stop to recognize or confront what is causing the tension. Extreme fear can transform into anxiety.

- Anger - Teens tend to be looked at as just naturally moody. They can snap and become angry in a matter of seconds for what seems to be no apparent reason. Navigating the teenage years leads to experiencing a number of big emotions and social situations that many are ill-equipped to confront. The most natural response for a teen is to lash out in anger. Teens are often looking for more independence but struggle with having to follow their parent's rules to a T. More is expected of them, yet less is offered to them in terms of being allowed more luxuries or freedoms. This anger can quickly turn into long periods of frustration or can result in feelings of hopelessness. As with any emotion, is a natural response, anger can make us act out in unpleasant and unwanted ways. Anger can get the best of you and make you do things you regret. When we respond in the

moment of anger, we often act in a way that is opposite of our values.

Anger can be a coping technique you have unintentionally picked up. Instead of dealing and feeling what you are really feeling, you may just default to anger. Often, when you sit and look at your anger, you may uncover that is it actually sadness, fear, or disappointment you are feeling and only covering it up with anger.

- Sadness - The teenage years are unfair. Greater expectations are placed on teens that may lead them to feel more disappointed. One of the most common ways for teens to deal with sadness is to withdraw. Sadness can make you feel unmotivated to live up to your potential, socialize, participate in activities, or simply do what you know is expected or that you should be doing. Long periods and frequently feeling sad can lead to feelings of becomes melancholy and depression.

- Joy - Joy is a form of happiness. When things are going well, we will feel more joy. There can be spikes in your moments of joy that can leave you in a state of euphoria. Joy can be fueled through gratitude. When we are able to be thankful for what we have and encounter, we are able to find more joy in the things we do.

- Disgust - Disgust is a negative feeling in which we often disagree or disprove of what is happening or feel a strong need to avoid what we are encountering. Long periods of disgust or exposure to these unpleasant encounters can transform into

hate, annoyance, and loathing. You can feel disgust because of others either because of their actions or words or you can feel disgust for yourself in the way you act, the way you look, or what you have done.

How to Manage Our Moods in Our Favor

To gain better control over your moods, you want to be able to identify what you are feeling. Your thoughts and feelings at the present moment will help you identify the mood you are in. You can do this by simply taking the time to just stop and ask yourself what you are feeling and why. When you notice that your feelings are not suited for the situation you are facing, you can begin to recognize when you need to make adjustments or further evaluate what you are thinking.

Once you are able to state to yourself what you are feeling, you can accept it. Whatever emotion or mood you do uncover, remind yourself that it is normal and OK to feel whatever way you are feeling. What you want to avoid doing is getting stuck on these moods. Instead of allowing your mood to hijack your day, you can acknowledge it and choose to move past what you are feeling.

You can learn to adjust the way you feel to better suit the situation you are facing or in. For instance, you might feel anxious and insecure about competing at a track meet or science fair. But this is not the way you want to feel. You want to feel confident, excited, and alert. You can recognize that the mood you are in is not beneficial, and you can shift it to better suit what you want to accomplish.

Exercises

Mood Awareness

How do the major emotions feel in your body?

What parts of your body are affected when you feel certain emotions?

What urges do you have when you are going through these emotions?

How long do you feel these sensations in your body?

Chapter 8: Boost Your Self-Esteem

How you view yourself affects what you pursue in your life. It affects what you will tolerate from others and will allow you to set and keep boundaries in place. There are many ways your self-esteem can impact your behavior and is a direct result of the way you view and think about yourself.

What Is Self-Esteem?

Self-esteem is a positive factor that can give you the confidence to achieve goals, form better relationships, have a positive outlook, and can bring your overall more satisfaction and happiness in all you do. During the teenage years, a young adult's self-esteem will reach phenomenal highs and depressing lows. Because of the many factors that can affect one's self-esteem, it is vital that teens learn to build themselves up and believe in their abilities despite what others may think, say, or how others respond or react to them.

Self-esteem can affect how we relate to others and how we value yourself. Self-esteem can impact physical and mental health. Those who develop low self-esteem are more likely to suffer from anxiety, stress, depression, and have more struggles with substance abuse. Those who have higher self-esteem will place more value on their own strengths and are not constantly seeking approval from others.

When a teen has higher self-esteem, they are able to assert themselves more and are willing and unafraid of trying new things and understand how their actions can have an impact on the world around them. This allows them to

make choices that align their behavior in a way that increases their self-esteem.

What Influences Self-Esteem?

There are a number of factors that can increase or decrease your self- esteem. Self-esteem can be affected by:

- Friends - Who we spend the most time with have the most impact on how we view ourselves. Those who have friends that are bad influences will often suffer from lower self-esteem as these friends can cause them to get into more trouble or feed into the negative thoughts they may already hold about themselves.

Even individuals who aren't considered friends will have a significant impact on self-esteem. Having to deal with bullies and give in to peer pressure can cause a teen to feel bad about themselves.

- Family life - Teens who have supportive parents and what is considered a more functional home life will often have higher self-esteem. When the home provides structure and encouragement, a teen will have more positive thoughts and experiences, and this will result in thinking more positively about who they are as a person and what they are capable of. Teens who face unsupportive, overly critical, or absent parents will develop a more negative view on themselves.

- School and work - If a teen has unrealistic expectations imposed on them regarding how they perform in school or at work, they can often feel disappointed. When constantly facing this disappointment, their self-esteem can plummet. They can

begin to identify and form irrational beliefs based on other people's expectations.

- How we react to others - Social interaction also plays a role in self-esteem at a young age. How you behave in front of others can strengthen or decrease how you feel about yourself. If you are always acting a certain way because of the attention it gets from others, you begin to feel as though you are unable to be who you truly are and fear that others may not like you if you are yourself.

How you respond to the way others treat you can impact your self-esteem. If you constantly react in a defensive manner, this is often a result of low self-esteem. If you find that you are unable to stick up for yourself or voice your own opinions, this is also a clear indication of low self-esteem.

- How we compare ourselves to others - Constantly comparing yourself to others is the fastest way to decrease self-esteem. For teens, it is almost impossible to avoid comparing yourself with others. You compare your looks, grades, friends, material objects, and everything else with those around you. This will not only decrease your self-esteem, but it can lead to constantly feeling inadequate or that you are lacking. This turns into anxiety and depression.

Additionally, social media, the news, and technology are having a bigger impact on a teen's self-esteem than ever before.

Self-esteem is not a static belief. As we go through different experiences and grow, the way we view ourselves will change and adjust to different circumstances and experiences. Having a healthy

balance of knowing and believing in what we are capable of as well as acknowledging the areas we can improve on will allow teens to excel not just in their teen years but throughout their adult years as well.

Low Self-Esteem

Low self-esteem makes us feel uncomfortable with ourselves and therefore makes us feel uncomfortable around others.

When a teen suffers from low self-esteem, they are often overwhelmed with self- critical thoughts, and this feeds into making poor decisions. They will often fall into a cycle of making bad choices, which is followed by harsh judgments from parents, teachers, or peers. They process negative thought after negative thought, and this leads them to feel inadequate. Then the cycle repeats continuously, and they never actually learn from the mistakes they made that started the whole process in the first place.

Your thoughts directly affect the way you view yourself, and this affects your behaviors and emotions significantly. When you feel as though you are not as good, smart, capable, or deserving as those around you, you will feel constantly let down, sad, and uneasy when you are with the people you call your friends. When we have low self-esteem, we tend to focus on the negative.

- You only notice your flaws.
- Your self-worth is lower.
- You feel incompetent.
- You feel what makes you unique is a curse.
- You do not take notice of your strengths.
- You feel unworthy of attention or love.
- You are not able to accept compliments.
- You stay in the background.
- You feel more sad or alone.

- You may become aggressive.
- You may be more irritable.

Having low self-esteem can often make you feel as though you are always putting on a show, like you are an imposter and that those around you will figure out that you are not as smart, fun, or enjoyable as you pretend to be. These feelings will affect the relationship you form, and they can lead to you making decisions for other people's approval instead of what you know to be morally right. These feelings also make it more challenging to try new things because you always fear how you will look or what others will think of you. You will turn down or avoid leadership roles or positions and keep you from excelling in the classroom, extracurricular activities, and much more.

For Parents:

You may notice that your teen is suffering from low self-esteem if:

- Your teen talks about being bullied in school.
- Your teen may go out of their way to avoid discussing problems they are having at school.
- Your teen becomes ill more often.
- You notice your teen avoids going out with friends more.
- Your teen begins hanging out with new friends that are a bad influence.

- You notice your teen feeling depressed.
- Your teen ignores what you are saying or ignores punishments imposed because of bad behavior.

Those with low self-esteem are more likely to suffer from mental disorders such as anxiety and depression. For those with lower self- esteem, being able to feel confident and comfortable in front of others

is a huge challenge, which is often due to focusing too much on what others think or fearing judgments from those around them.

High Self-Esteem

Those with high self-esteem are often able to look at things realistically. They take responsibility for their successes and failures and are able to bounce back when they encounter disappointment. They don't overreact to situations. If they fail a test, they examine all the factors, and as a result, are able to conclude that they failed because they didn't study thoroughly. They don't think of themselves as not smart or as a failing student. They learn from the mistake of not studying and move forward knowing what to do better next time.

Keep in mind that while you want to have high self-esteem, there is a fine line from crossing over into narcissism. When individuals have too much self-esteem, they may believe that they do not need to improve on anything in their life. They can come off as being self-centered, develop beliefs of entitlement, and never learn from their failures. While high self-esteem is necessary to succeed, not admitting or taking responsibility for things that occur in your life will be a hindrance.

Those who have high self-esteem:

- Understand that confidence is not the same as arrogance.
- Welcome constructive criticism.
- Do not need to please everyone.
- Are not looking for approval.
- Can confront conflict in a healthy manner.
- Set boundaries in their life.
- Can express their needs and opinions in an effective way.
- Are assertive but not pushy.
- Do not strive for perfectionism.
- Can overcome setbacks.
- Can learn from their failures.
- Never feel as though they are inferior to others.
- Are comfortable with who they are.

How We Evaluate Ourselves

If we constantly feel as though we are not equal to or as good as those we surround ourselves with, this will often affect the effort we put into studying, making the right choices, and simply trying out for the things we would truly enjoy participating in a sport or scholarship. Your behaviors will align with the way you think about yourself and what you feel you are capable of.

If you are highly critical of yourself, you may never give yourself the credit you deserve or need to succeed in life. Unfortunately, most of the time we evaluate ourselves, it is in comparison to how others perform against us. Some of these comparisons are based on physical features; others are internal comparisons. When we focus our attention on external comparisons such as worrying about what others think, then we have an increase in self-worth instability. These instabilities increase the risk of depression and unwelcome behaviors. If we learn to make internal comparisons and learn to improve ourselves based on our own accomplishments and abilities, there is less instability, and self-esteem is easier to increase.

Other People's View and the Effect on Our Self-Esteem

When teens are faced with constant disapproval from others, such as their parents, teachers, or peers, they will often develop low self- esteem. But those who already have higher self-esteem are able to accept this disapproval and use it to improve themselves. They do not get caught up on other people's reactions and they do not put all their value or self-worth in the opinions or approval of others.

Social Comparison

Social comparison is the process in which we evaluate ourselves and accomplished against those around us. This type of comparison can affect our social and personal worth. Social media has made it easier than ever to observe and formulate assumptions based on what we see others sharing with the world. Many teens turn to social media to updates and posts from their peers, which can result in a constant state of comparing themselves to others.

Social comparison can be used as a way to acknowledge areas or things you want to improve in yourself; they can be used to motivate you to make improvements, and they can help you develop a more healthy or positive self-image. Unfortunately, social comparison often causes a teen to only focus on their flaws or bring about negative thoughts over never being able to reach the level another peer may be at.

Self-Observation Process

Self-observation is a process in which you focus on yourself in a non- judgmental way. People able to look inside yourself and notice your thoughts, emotions, and behaviors can help you increase your own self-esteem. Self-observation is a way for you to reflect on what makes you unique. It is a way to identify where negative thoughts, beliefs, and behaviors are affecting the way you view yourself or how you want to view yourself. This process allows you to debunk the negative identity that has been formed through social comparison and other feelings of inadequacy.

Cognitive Inferences

Cognitive inferences are what occurs when we form ideas about ourselves with no real evidence to back up these ideas. Also referred to as arbitrary interpretation or arbitrary inferences, we interpret a situation or experience and come to a conclusion about ourselves without considering all the evidence. Focusing on what other people think of us without actually having any clue as to what they are thinking is the most common way we form these types of inferences. We may automatically think that no one likes us or that everyone thinks we are a loser, but in reality, we have no way of knowing what others are thinking. When we form ideas without evidence, we tend to have lower self-esteem.

Selective Abstractions

Selective abstractions are the result of magnifying small negative details that we then use as a foundation to represent who we are. When we evaluate ourselves in this manner, we ignore any positive feedback or positive reinforcements; we only focus on the negative details. These small negative details are then exaggerated. and the way we view ourselves can be completely altered. Selective abstraction causes us to narrow in on negative feedback or reactions from others, and this reaction fuels all the negativity we might feel about ourselves. Even if there is evidence that supports the opposite thoughts, we dismiss the positive evidence. When we evaluate ourselves through selective abstractions, we immediately feel negative about ourselves.

How to Increase Low Self-Esteem

When you are able to identify areas in your life that bring on negative or unwanted thoughts, you can begin to change your through pattern, and in turn, change your behavior so that you can take a chance on more opportunities. By doing this, you will see the way you view yourself changes.

When it comes to increasing self-esteem, the best place to begin is to identify what is causing the low self-esteem to begin with. Oftentimes, negative self-talk and feelings of inadequacy are the root cause of low self-esteem.

One way you can begin to work through this negative self-talk and inadequacy is to recognize that these arise because of how we think others perceive us, not because of who we really are. Work to change those negatives into more positive and affirming statements.

Your self-esteem will begin to improve when you are able to feel more confident in your abilities, talk to your self more positively, and are able to take responsibility for your own actions.

For Parents:

Remember that the way a teen speaks to themselves is often a mirror of how they are being spoken to. If you ridicule your teen because they forgot to do a chore you asked them to do and back up these statements with negative views of them, such as them being lazy or inconsiderate, this only reinforces their low self-esteem.

1. Problem Solving

Problem-solving is a skill teens will greatly benefit from developing earlier on. Since in their adult lives they will be faced with having to make a number of hard decisions and find solutions for their problems on their own this is something that needs to be practiced. Teens that are allowed to work through the decision making progress, test out a solution, and evaluate the results will learn how to effectively solve the many challenges they will be faced with more confidence.

When teens learn to solve problems on their own their self-esteem naturally increases. This is because they learn to feel empowered by the choices they make, even if the results are not what they had hoped for.

2.   Self-Talk

Positive self-talk is vital for high self-esteem. Adopting a more positive inner dialog can be challenging for teens as they are often confronted with harsh words from bullies, the media, and others. Being too critical can lead to limiting beliefs of feeling as though you will never accomplish anything, feeling as though you will never be good enough, and can result in teens becoming too eager and focused on being perfect or too discouraged to even try.

Improved self-talk is not something that will easily change overnight. Once you begin to recognize the negative self-talk, you can start to reword what you say so that the dialog that takes place in your head is one that encourages you to improve where you need to improve and to not get stuck on not accomplishing things the way you had anticipated them being done.

3.   Self-Control

How we behave in social settings has a lot to do with our self-control. Some teens are unaware of how to take control of their behaviors, and for other teens, anxiety clouds their ability to control themselves the way they know they should or would like to.

Practicing different social situations and modeling self-control behaving is an effective way for teens to learn and improve on their own self-control. The goal is to help your teen become more comfortable in social situations and more confident in their ability to respond in an appropriate way.

For Parents:

Here are some ways you can help boost your teens self-esteem:

•   Praise them for their accomplishments, no matter how small.

•   Give them credit when they are making an effort, even if the task they complete is not up to your own standards of how it should be done.

•   Turn mistakes into an opportunity for them to learn.

•   Point out negative self-talk and how they can reframe these to more empowering thoughts.

- Try new things with your teen.

- Allow them to make their own choices and have their own opinions without telling them they are wrong.

- Volunteer with your teen or encourage them to give back to others.

When giving praise, be specific about their accomplishments. Do not fall back on generic praise.

Self-Actualization

Once basic needs are met, like food, shelter, and cleaner air, individuals move on to acquire more fulfilling needs, such as feeling love, increasing self-worth, finding a place they belong, and feeling safe in their environment and with those around them. Self- actualization is the process we go through when we want to add more meaning to our lives through personal and social objectives. We meet these objectives through our creativity, intellectual expansion, and social progress.

Chapter 9: New Thoughts

You learned earlier how to identify your negative thoughts patterns. You learned how your beliefs and values can have an impact and also be affected by your thoughts. Changing the way you think is no easy task. Negative thoughts will creep into your mind and ruin your day if you are not aware of when they occur or how to combat them.

While identifying your thought patterns is the first step, transforming them to empower you will take practice. There are many ways you can shift your thinking. There are effective ways you can reinforce positive thoughts and behaviors that you can adopt to keep your thoughts and actions in line with who you are and who you want to become. Refer back to what your values are. Your values can help you keep your thoughts aligned with what matters most to you.

Exercises

Affirmations

Create your own empowering "I am" statements. Make them personal and specific to the goals you want to achieve. Some examples:

- I am loved.
- I am a great friend.
- I am in control of my thoughts.
- I am working hard to improve my grades.
- I respect my parents, and they trust me to make the right choices.

Once you have your affirmations in writing, repeat them at least three times a day. Stand in front of a mirror and believe fully in what you are saying to yourself. Do this every day and notice how your behavior begins to change.

When you notice negative thoughts bombarding your mind, repeat these affirmations to stop the cycle and redirect the direction your thoughts go. Notice how your confidence increases, how you approach others differently, and how you treat yourself. Every week, take some time to look over these affirmations and create news ones when necessary. The most important component in writing these affirmations is that you constantly repeat them to yourself. Your negative thought patterns will be disrupted, and your brain will begin to change the way it processes your experience and allow you to have more positive views on what you face and a more positive view on

yourself. The more you practice positive self-talk, the more your thoughts will change.

Write your affirmations now.

Create a Let It Go Phrase

Negative thoughts will come and go throughout your day. There is no way to completely eliminate them, but there are ways you can disrupt your typical thought pattern and stop the negative thoughts in their tracks. Instead of giving extra attention and energy to your negative thoughts, have a go-to phrase that allows you to acknowledge then but then simply let them go. This works well when you notice thought that involves a limited or negative belief.

For example:

You notice the negative belief of "I am not good at anything" creep up on you.

You can address this thought by simply stating "Oh, hey that's just nonsense" or "Wow, I can't believe I used to believe that" or "But there are so many things I haven't even tried yet; this cannot be true".

You are adding a bit of humor but also making it known that this thought has no evidence to back it up.

Think of some of the common negative thoughts or beliefs you notice occur regularly. Now, think of a phrase you can say to yourself that will oppose this thought and allow you to see the nonsense of the statement.

You can write it out like this.

Negative thought/belief:

Counter phrase:

Shift to a Growth Mindset

One of the easiest things you can start implementing now to shift your fixed mindset to a growth mindset is to add the word "yet" at the end of those limiting phrases.

- "I'm not good at playing the drums, yet".
- "I'm not fast enough to play football, yet."
- "I am not good with grammar, yet."

Adding "yet" to the end of these phrases immediately begins to shift your fixed mindset to a growth mindset. When you find yourself focused on what you can't do now, add "yet" to what you say to yourself.

Chapter 10: New Behaviors

Behaviors become habitual the more we act on them. Our behaviors are our reaction to internal or external stimuli. How we perceive ourselves, our values, beliefs, and mindset can influence our behaviors and vice versa. When we notice an inconsistency in our behaviors and what we want to be, we can address and change so that everything aligns correctly. Social and peer pressure are the two most common factors that cause our behaviors to act out of line with who we want to be.

Recognize the Behaviors You Want to Change

Some behaviors will not necessarily fall into the category of aligning with your values, but they can be destructive or unhelpful. These behaviors, such as impulsively texting, yelling, or not doing homework, are behaviors you may simply want to decrease or stop. To rid yourself of these behaviors, you have to first be able to notice them as they occur in your daily life. You will want to track these behaviors for two to three days and list the times they occur, the places they occur, and who you are with. The point of tracking isn't to stop yourself at this point from the behavior; instead, you want to know when they are most likely to occur so that you can come up with an alternative behavior to do.

This is challenging as most children are not told what to do; they are only told what not to do from an early age: "Stop running", "don't touch," "no hitting." While this reinforces that you are not supposed to do something, this doesn't direct you to what you are actually supposed to do. Instead, instructions such as "Walk "or "slow down," "keep your hands to your side," "nice hands" are more helpful. While you can identify what you may not want to be doing, the only way you can stop the behavior is if you know what you want to replace the behavior with.

Exercise

- List three behaviors you would like to decrease or stop.

1.

2.

3.

- Track when these behaviors occur for two to three days.

1.

2.

3.

- List two replacement behaviors for each instance you notice they occur. You can repeat the replacement behavior as many times for different situations as you are able to.

If listing two replacement behaviors is a challenge, then at least come up with two replacement behaviors for each behavior you want to change and use this as a starting point for coming up with more replacement behaviors that can be beneficial in different settings.

Behaviors That Are Beneficial But You Avoid

There may be behaviors you want to adopt but your fear or anxiety holds you back from attempting them. Since you have gone through some of the steps and exercises in conquering your anxiety, you may find that you have more confidence in trying to incorporate more beneficial behaviors. To overcome and adopt new behaviors you avoid out of fear, take steps to gradually become more comfortable in the situations that involve this behavior.

For example:

If you want to participate more in class but have avoided doing so because you fear public speaking, you may begin by simply talking to your teacher or participating in small group discussions more. Over time, you may raise your hand once a week to answer a question, then move up to once a day.

If you fear giving a presentation in class, you might begin by again discussing the presentation with other classmates. Then, you might practice giving the presentation when you are alone, then in front of your family, then friends. The more you practice, the more comfortable and confident you will be in the situation. By practicing, you also allow yourself to stop the negative thoughts you have associated with the behavior you have been avoiding.

Exercise:

- List the behaviors that you want to begin to incorporate into your life that you have been avoiding up until now out of fear or anxiety.

- List how these behaviors can be beneficial for you in the long- term.

Positive Reinforcement

Positive reinforcement is essential when it comes to adopting new behaviors. We are more likely to continue to do something when we are getting something out of it, whether it is because the reward aligns with our values, thoughts, or personal preferences. Think about all the behaviors you exhibit throughout the day.

- Helping your friends

- Dong chores
- Finishing your homework
- Being on time for work

Now consider the reasons why you do these things; what do you get out of them?

- Being considered a good friend
- Gaining praise or more independence from your parents
- Getting good grades
- Being viewed as a good employee

There are many behaviors throughout the day you seemingly do by default, but you actually do them because there is some kind of a reward in it for you. When you are trying to change behaviors or begin new ones, one of the first things you can use as motivation is having a simple reward system in place. You want to create a list of positive reinforcements that will help keep you moving in the right direction.

- Buying a new pair of shoes
- Buying a new game
- Watching a new TV series
- Getting your hair done

The reward has to be something that will motivate you and that you won't be able to access until you have successfully adopted the new behaviors.

Exercise:

List the ways you can reward yourself.

Accountability

It is easier for us to follow through on what we promise to others than it is to follow through on what we promise ourselves. When you enlist a close family member or friend to keep you accountable, there is a higher chance that you will be successful simply because you don't want to let the other person down. It is also to have someone in on your goals that you can celebrate your victories with.

Exercise:

List some individuals you can go to for accountability.

Chapter 11: Creating New Objectives?

Setting goals or objectives will help assist you in building confidence and change your negative thinking patterns. Once you have achieved one goal, creating another can be easily done and accomplished. Look back on the previous chapters and take into consideration:

1. The areas of your life you want to see the most progress in.

2. The core beliefs you want to change.

3. The values that are important to you.

4. The negative thought patterns that may create obstacles.

Looking over each of these areas will help you formulate new objectives and create a plan for accomplishing your goals.

Steps for Creating New Objectives

1. Refer back to your value pyramid.
2. Start with the most important value.
3. Come up with a goal that supports this value.

4.   What steps do you need to take to achieve this goal?

5.   What is the first step you are going to take? Keep in mind:

1.   What are some barriers or obstacles that you may face as you work through each step? (These barriers can also be the negative thoughts that might arise as you progress toward your goal.)

2.   What are some solutions that will help you overcome these obstacles?

Why Set New Objectives?

Goals allow you to have a clear vision of where we are going and what we are working toward. When you set effective goals, you can more easily navigate the road before you and set yourself up for success despite the obstacles you may encounter. The goals you set will allow you to determine if the steps you are taking are actually helpful and moving you to where you want to be.

When thinking of your goals, ensure that they are specific, achievable, important, and realistic.

Creating an Action Plan

To set a goal, think about the following questions:

1. What is the first value you want to commit to working toward?

2. What goals align with this value?

3.   What behaviors do you want to change, stop, or incorporate that align with the value?

4.   What specific goal do you want to reach that will help you with these new behaviors?

These goals should be short-term and easy to accomplish. For example, if you want to start exercising, your goal could be to exercise two times that week.

Working in weekly increments will make it easier for you to track your progress and even easier to achieve.

Write out your specific goals for this upcoming week now.

Now, let's put everything together so you can create a plan that is easy to follow.

Date: /   /   Goal:

Times and days you plan to work on this goal:

Write the name of those who are keeping you accountable:

Write your positive reinforcement or the reward you will treat yourself with once this goal has been accomplished for the week.

You will do the same plan for the next week, only this time you will review your progress from the previous week. What goals did you struggle with that you will need to come up with a solution for (what barriers or obstacles did you run into while you were trying to accomplish this goal)?

Are there any goals that you swap out for the next-step goals (if one of your goals was to find a job, and the first step was to do a job search, the next step may be getting applications or setting up an interview)?

Were your rewards appealing enough?

Are there some behaviors you can increase the times you do them in the week (instead of working out two days a week, work out three)?

Conclusion

Being a teenager is not easy. Handling big emotions, negative thoughts, and out-of-control behaviors are not easy. As a teenager, you might be trying your best to act the way you are expected, to get the grades you are expected to, and participate in other activities that you expected to participate in. There are a lot of expectations.

It is no wonder that many teens suffer from anxiety, depression, and other disorders that leave them feeling helpless. It is also no surprise that these feelings of helplessness result in behaviors that make them feel in control even though they are not the best behaviors. And, it is also no surprise that these feelings and behaviors are what they will carry on in their adult life.

Your teen years will only last a few years, but what occurs during these years will stay with you for the rest of your life. Adopting a more positive outlook on yourself, those around you, and the world around you can result in great success once you reach adulthood.

Cognitive Behavioral Therapy is one way that you can begin to stop the limiting beliefs and views you have on yourself. This book offers you an introduction to the steps you can take to have more control over your emotions, thoughts, and behaviors.

Continue to utilize the tips, techniques, and tools described in the chapters when you trying to make a big decision or improve grades, when you are trying to strengthen your relationships and increase your confidence.

References

Bialasiewicz, K. (2017, December 17). Moods and Emotions: How to Tell the Difference and Make Changes. Retrieved from http://timhillpsychotherapy.com/moods-vs-emotions/.

Chansard, T., & Tikkou, F. (2019). Conquer anxiety workbook for teens: find peace from worry, panic, fear, and phobias. Althea Press.

Gavin, M. L. (Ed.). (n.d.). Choosing Your Mood (for Teens) - Nemours KidsHealth. Retrieved from https://kidshealth.org/en/teens/choose- mood.html.

Sussex Publishers. (n.d.). How Do You Evaluate Your Self-Worth? Retrieved from

https://www.psychologytoday.com/us/blog/emotional-nourishment/201804/how-do-you-evaluate-your-self-worth.

History of Cognitive Behavior Therapy - CBT: Beck Institute. (n.d.). Retrieved from https://beckinstitute.org/about-beck/team/our- history/history-of-cognitive-therapy/.

Hutt, R. L. (2019). Feeling better: Cbt workbook for teens: essential skills and activities to help you manage moods, boost self-esteem, and conquer anxiety. Althea Press.

JOSEFOWITZ, N. I. N. A. (2020). Cbt Made Simple: a clinician's guide to practicing cognitive behavioral therapy.

NEW HARBINGER PUB. Sussex Publishers. (n.d.). Personal Growth: Your Values, Your Life. Retrieved from https://www.psychologytoday.com/us/blog/the-power-prime/201205/personal-growth-your-values-your-life.

www.ingramcontent.com/pod-product-compliance
Lightning Source LLC
Chambersburg PA
CBHW071623080526
44588CB00010B/1241